In Praise of
Renewed Federalism

Thomas J. Courchene

The Canada Round:
A Series on the Economics of
Constitutional Renewal — No. 2

John McCallum, Series Editor

C.D. Howe Institute

C.D. Howe Institute publications are available from:

Renouf Publishing Company Limited, 1294 Algoma Road,
Ottawa, Ontario K1B 3W8; phone (613) 741-4333; fax (613) 741-5439

and from Renouf's stores at:

61 Sparks Street, Ottawa (613) 238-8985
211 Yonge Street, Toronto (416) 363-3171

For trade book orders, please contact:

McGraw-Hill Ryerson Limited, 300 Water Street,
Whitby, Ontario L1N 9B6; phone (416) 430-5050

Institute publications are also available in microform from:

Micromedia Limited, 20 Victoria Street, Toronto, Ontario M5C 2N8

This book is printed on recycled, acid-free paper.

Canadian Cataloguing in Publication Data

Courchene, Thomas J., 1940–
    In praise of renewed federalism

(The Canada round, ISSN 1049-3210 ; no. 2)
ISBN 0-88806-282-6

1. Quebec (Province) – History – Autonomy and independence.
2. Federal-provincial relations – Canada.* 3. Federal government – Canada.
I. C.D. Howe Institute. II. Title. III. Series.

FC2925.9.S37C68 1991   320.471'049   C91-094765-1
F1053.2.C68 1991

73806

Contents

Foreword

Canada appears poised to embark on an historic political recon-figuration. It is essential that this process be undertaken with a clear and widely diffused understanding of the well-spring of Canadians' economic prosperity.

It is with that in mind that the C.D. Howe Institute presents this series of monographs entitled *The Canada Round*. The series assembles the work of many of Canada's leading economic and political analysts. The monographs are organized into two groups. The first group, called "The Economics of Constitutional Renewal", rests on the assumption of renewed federalism and is organized around economic themes. It examines the economic goals that Canadians have set for themselves, as well as the means of achieving them and the influence of alternative constitutional structures.

The second group of studies, called "Breakup", examines the economic consequences of Quebec independence for both Quebec and the rest of Canada. A unique feature of the "Breakup" studies is that they will be integrated with the research that has already been carried out by Quebec's Bélanger-Campeau Commission. Where appropriate, each of the studies in this group will include a summary of the relevant analysis by the Bélanger-Campeau Commission, contributions by experts from across Canada, as well as shorter critiques or replies. This format, we believe, will help to pierce Canada's "several solitudes" and create a pan-Canadian meeting of minds.

The Canada Round is not intended to alarm or frighten — the process of collective political definition in this country will turn on more than simply questions of dollars and cents. And, as these monographs will reveal, economics rarely produces an open-and-shut case as to the superiority of one possible set of rules over another. Even if it could do this, it would be unwise to assume that economic analysis alone could change the minds of those who are already committed to a particular vision of the political future.

It is equally clear, however, that Canadians are now seeking a greater understanding of the links between the economy, the Constitution, and legal and political life. A significant reform of the Constitution will influence the economy, in some cases for the better; a rending of the Constitution under conditions of acrimony will almost certainly damage it. Thus, the purpose of the series is to help Canadians think constructively about the benefits and costs of alternative constitutional designs.

Underlying the series is a focus on the economic well-being of Canadians, now and in the future. To best insure this well-being over the short run, Canada needs calm, open negotiations in which efforts are made to understand and incorporate the aspirations of all the participants. This series of monographs is dedicated to that effort.

John McCallum, the series editor and Chairman of the Department of Economics at McGill University, organized the intellectual input. Within the C.D. Howe Institute, David Brown, Senior Policy Analyst, played a coordinating role. This second monograph in the series was copy edited and prepared for publication by Barry A. Norris. As with all C.D. Howe Institute publications, the analysis and views presented here are the responsibility of the author and do not necessarily reflect the opinions of the Institute's members or Board of Directors.

Thomas E. Kierans
President and
Chief Executive Officer

The Study in Brief

In this second volume of "The Canada Round", the C.D. Howe Institute's new series on the economics of constitutional renewal, Professor Thomas J. Courchene analyzes three options for the future of Canada and Quebec: (1) an economic and monetary union between the two; (2) complete independence for Quebec, accompanied by free trade agreements between Quebec and "the Rest of Canada" (ROC) and Quebec and the United States; and (3) renewed federalism.

Option 1: A Canada-Quebec Economic and Monetary Union

Courchene argues that this option may well be the worst of the three. It is likely to be unfeasible on either political or economic grounds, as well as undesirable from the standpoints of both Quebec and ROC.

Drawing on current experience in the European Community, Courchene suggests that the political process embodied in Canada's present federal system or in any form of renewed federalism would offer Quebec more genuine sovereignty than would any economic and monetary union governed by administrative and legal processes. Courchene's argument includes the following points:

- If Quebec's status under the current Canada-U.S. Free Trade Agreement were to shift from that of a province to that of a sovereign nation, it would become less free to follow its own distinctive policies in a number of important areas, including: the regulation of financial institutions; its present European-style approach to the integration of the financial and real sectors ("Quebec Inc."); Hydro-Québec's pricing of electricity; the "subsidies" offered to Quebec companies by the Caisse de dépôt; and procurement by both the Quebec government and Hydro-Québec.

- Notwithstanding the "principle of subsidiarity", European experience suggests that a viable economic and monetary union requires the concentration of a great deal of regulatory power at the center. Examples include rigid environmental standards, tough rules governing procurement policies and subsidies, and restrictions on government deficits, bailouts, and foreign borrowing.

- All of these rules would reduce Quebec's ability to respond to economic shocks. In addition, the cushions that the federal government now provides through unemployment insurance, equalization payments, and so on would no longer exist.

Courchene also points out that bipolar confederal systems with important policymaking functions are inherently unstable when the two partners are of unequal size. Either Quebec would have to have veto power, which would be unacceptable to ROC, or the decisions would have to be dominated by ROC, which would be unacceptable to Quebec.

Yet even if such an arrangement were feasible, Quebec would not want it, Courchene argues, because it would give the province less sovereignty than it now has. It would emasculate Quebec society of its innate advantage of being a North American economy with a distinctive non-North American approach to political economy. A full-fledged economic and monetary union would result in a greater, rather than a reduced, entanglement between Quebec and ROC, which is certainly not what the emerging "let Quebec go" mentality in ROC has in mind.

Option 2: Quebec Independence without an Economic and Monetary Union

This option, Courchene says, is likely to involve free trade agreements between Quebec and both ROC and the United States, and a system in which Quebec "uses" the Canadian dollar as its own currency. The problem here is that the economic risks are extraordinarily high, not only for Quebec but for ROC as well. The transition period could be extremely long and costly, and ROC's continuing political integrity could be called into question.

Option 3: Renewed Federalism

This is Courchene's preferred route. He notes that Quebec has two sets of demands: first, a restructuring of Canadian institutions in a manner that is consistent with improving the ability of this country to compete successfully in a rapidly globalizing world economy; and, second, additional powers, mainly in the area of "demolinguistics". Courchene argues that these demands can and should be met. The first is not only an economic challenge but also an opportunity that all Canadians should embrace regardless of the country's future political structure. As to the second, Courchene emphasizes the flexibility of Canada's federal system and the demonstrated genius of Canadians in fashioning innovative solutions, frequently without the need for formal constitutional amendments. Courchene concludes:

> All Canadians will want to embrace a Canada that reorganizes itself to be a "winner", since it is only within this context that Canadians can sustain the socio-cultural vision of their country that is gradually becoming the late 20th- century version of the last century's "national dream" of an east-west railway. Indeed, they will embrace such a Canada enthusiastically.

John McCallum
Series Editor

Acknowledgments

I would like to acknowledge the valuable comments on an earlier draft from my colleague John McDougall and from Marcel Côté of Secor. My greatest debt, however, is to Tom Kierans, not only in matters of substance but also in terms of timely encouragement during the preparation of the monograph. Responsibility for the views that follow rests with me. This paper replaces a much earlier draft entitled "The Integration Requisites of a Canadian Economic and Monetary Union: Lessons from the European Community."

Thomas J. Courchene
Kingston, Ontario
May 1991

Chapter 1

Introduction and Overview

Canada is now "in play". Stunned and humiliated by the rejection of the Meech Lake Accord, Quebecers have now attached themselves, emotionally and politically, in growing numbers to the sovereignty option. In order to make this choice more economically palatable, they have latched onto the scenario of economic association or "political superstructure", having in mind the European Community (EC) as a model. Specifically, both the Parti Québécois' (PQ) first-best option and the default option contained in the Allaire Report[1] involve a declaration of sovereignty or independence to be then followed by an economic and monetary union with "the Rest of Canada" (ROC).

Meanwhile, in the immediate post-Meech Lake era, ROC embarked on a research agenda falling under the rubric of "reconstituted federalism"; for a while, debating the pros and cons of symmetric versus asymmetric federalism was all the rage. But ROC was equally stunned by the dramatic nature of the Allaire Report. In this context, the Bélanger-Campeau Report is largely anticlimactic, focusing as it does principally on process.[2] The real thrust of the Bélanger-Campeau Report is in its background documents, which, because they exist only in French, will filter into ROC only very slowly, if at all.

---

1   Quebec Liberal Party, Constitutional Committee, *A Quebec Free to Choose* (Quebec, January 28, 1991), usually referred to as the "Allaire Report" after the Committee's Chairman, Jean Allaire.

2   See Quebec, Commission on the Political and Constitutional Future of Quebec, *Report* (Quebec, March 27, 1991), usually referred to as the "Bélanger-Campeau Report" after the Commission's co-chairmen, Michel Bélanger and Jean Campeau.

To say that ROC has been humiliated by the conclusions contained in these two reports is probably not accurate. What is emerging in ROC, however, is a "let them go" or "bon voyage" mentality that is reflected — at least in part — in the dramatic recent rise in popularity of the Reform Party. Moreover, this hardening of attitudes on the part of ROC toward any and all of Quebec's demands is accompanied by an incredible emphasis on process, particularly of the constituent assembly variety — so much so that at times it appears that process is becoming the substance of the constitutional debate in ROC.

The net result is that the constitutional debate is not being joined. Rather, Quebec and ROC are turning inward and, in effect, feeding on the "two solitudes". This is the "constitutional" aspect of the crisis that Canada now faces. With it goes the fear — and the very real possibility — that, consciously or unconsciously, this country's political integrity might be torn apart. Perhaps it is best to refer to this as the "political aspect" of the crisis.

What is only beginning to emerge is a quite different perspective of the underlying challenge — one that has to do with Canada's economic viability into the next century and beyond. The issues here revolve around:

- halting this country's competitive decline;
- getting on stride with globalization and the telecomputational revolution;
- grappling with Canada's internal "transfer dependency", which is sapping the innovation and viability of an increasing number of provinces;
- placing the fiscal structures at *all* levels of government on a more sustainable basis;
- promoting and developing Canadians' human capital both for its own sake and in recognition that knowledge is an essential part of the key to competitiveness in the new world economy.

To be sure, the Allaire Report highlighted this economic aspect of the crisis when it effectively proclaimed that Canada no longer works economically. But this perspective has so far been overwhelmed in Quebec by the political and constitutional dimensions of the debate, and it has yet to really surface in ROC. It will soon do so, however, and in my view it will eventually come to dominate much of the constitutional aspect of the crisis.

After nearly two decades of looking inward while the rest of the world was passing them by, Canadians will finally broach the globalization imperative in their debate on national unity. In an important sense, this aspect of the ongoing challenge to Canada is one of "economic opportunity". In order for this perception of the impasse to come to the fore, it is essential that the constitutional aspect of the crisis be dealt with first. Therefore, this study of necessity focuses largely on the constitutional and political arrangements, with only selective emphasis on what promises to emerge as the much more critical set of economic and social policy issues as Canada moves toward the 21st century.

The thrust of the ensuing analysis is that, in pursuing the constitutional and political dimension of the crisis, both parties are courting not only economic disaster but in all likelihood political disaster as well. For Quebec — a province that has carefully orchestrated its economic evolution over the past 30 years and in the process maneuvered brilliantly within the limits imposed by the Constitution and Canadian federalism — the fundamental question is: Why would it risk its economic — and perhaps its cultural — future by opting for independence only to immediately hand back to some confederal economic and monetary union superstructure much of its newly gained *and existing* powers? Is there not a preferable economic and political/cultural future for Quebec within a renewed federalism? My answer is yes.

For ROC, the question is similar: Why is it apparently willing to subject both its economic future and the likelihood that it can remain a united nation to the growing view that the current crisis presents an opportunity somehow to "disentangle" politically from Quebec and in the process to create a society that is more in its own likeness and image? Is there not a preferable economic and political future for ROC within a reconstituted Canada? Again, my answer is yes.

In full recognition that mere assertion carries, appropriately, no weight in our societal debate, this study attempts to document and demonstrate that to create two separate nations in the upper part of North America — with or without an economic and monetary union — is clearly a negative-sum economic (and likely political) game. My entrée into this analysis is to direct focus initially on Quebec and, in particular, on whether the European experience with an economic and a (proposed) monetary union provides a viable model for Quebec and ROC. Detailing the full range of opportunities and constraints associated with a Quebec-ROC economic and monetary union is absolutely essential in order to move the constitutional debate in Quebec from the political and emotional plane to an economic and strategic one. Not incidentally, this form of analysis can also be applied to ROC, since, of necessity, it highlights the range of costs and opportunities that would attend ROC in any "post-Canada" economic and monetary union.

To anticipate the analysis, I conclude that, with some caveats, a Quebec-ROC economic union is not feasible and probably not desirable. This is not necessarily good news for ROC, since I then go on to demonstrate that an independent Quebec linked by free trade agreements to ROC and to the United States is in some ways a more viable long-term "solution" for that province than a confederal political superstructure on the EC model. The problem with this particular constitutional game is that the transition is likely to be very costly, and not only for Quebec. With this analysis as backdrop, the final substantive chapter comes at renewed federalism from what I hope is a fresh vantage point — namely, as a potentially positive-sum game on both the political and economic fronts, in sharp contrast to the negative-sum attributes of the breakup scenarios.

Before detailing the structure of the study, I want to direct some initial attention to the economic and monetary union conception of "post-Canada", since it is at the core of Quebec's strategy and since it will play a central role in the ensuing analysis.

The Relevance of the European Experience: A First Glance

As I have already noted, the highest common denominator in terms of formal proposals emanating from Quebec appears to be sovereignty coupled with a pan-Canadian economic union and joint management of a Canadian currency. As also noted, this has long been the PQ's first-best option. The Allaire Report in its "default option" is equally clear: if the rest of Canada does not agree to the restructuring outlined in the report, then there ought to be a referendum before the fall of 1992 that would "propose that Quebec assume the status of a sovereign state [and that] in this case Quebec [would] offer to arrange an economic union with the rest of Canada, managed by institutions of a confederal nature." The Allaire Report's definition of an "economic union" includes both (a) free mobility of goods, people, and capital and (b) a customs and monetary union.[3]

This being the case, one can then pose the following question: What is the nature of the minimum political, institutional, and economic superstructure — that is, the minimum political and economic integration — consistent with the maintenance on a sustainable basis of a common currency and an economic union in the upper half of North America? Henceforth, I refer to this combination of a common currency and an economic union as a "Canada-Quebec economic and monetary union," or CQEMU for short.

Conveniently, this is *exactly* the question that the EC is asking itself as it moves beyond an economic union ("Europe 1992") and toward a single European currency and a single European central bank. I use "European economic and monetary union" (EEMU) to refer to the combination of a European economic union and a single

---

3 Allaire Report, pp. 59, 61. To these two precepts, the report adds a third factor that it deems essential to ensure a meaningful economic union — namely, "restoring balance to Canadian public finances by reducing the size of the central state and imposing institutional limitations on its budgetary practices, including the establishment of specific targets to severely limit deficits and restrict its taxation power" (p. 61). This aspect is elaborated on later in the study.

currency area. Thus, EEMU and CQEMU, as defined here, are similar concepts.

Intriguingly, and even more conveniently, if Quebec declares its independence and then seeks to establish (or re-establish) an economic and monetary union with ROC, not only do the Quebec and ROC situations fully parallel that of Europe, but the specific assumptions underlying reintegration are also fully parallel. Consider the three key assumptions driving Europe toward an EEMU:

- There will be a single European currency, backed up by a single central bank — that is, a "EuroFed", or some European version of the U.S. Federal Reserve System.
- There will be free movement of goods, services, capital, and persons across national boundaries — in other words, the Treaty of Rome *plus* "Europe 1992".
- The "principle of subsidiarity" will obtain. Essentially, this means that, unless there are dominating economic rationales to the contrary, powers will remain with national governments and not transferred upward to the Community level (see the box on the opposite page, which contains a brief outline of aspects of this principle).

As noted, these precepts fully parallel those of the PQ and the "fallback position" of the Allaire Report. In particular, the Allaire Report, drawing in large measure from the Quebec Chamber of Commerce's submission to the Bélanger-Campeau Commission, has bought fully into the "principle of subsidiarity" by suggesting that most powers should reside at the provincial ("member state") level. Part of the analysis here, then, attempts to address whether subsidiarity is a viable long-term principle or whether it will fall prey — triggered by outside influences and globalization — to an "expansionist bureaucratic dynamic" at the administrative center of the economic union, be that Brussels or Ottawa.

Thus, while the ensuing analysis focuses on Canada, it draws heavily on the EEMU experience and prospects. The tremendous advantage that this lends to the analysis of a CQEMU is that the

The Principle of Subsidiarity

The economic meaning of the principle of *subsidiarity*: assigning tasks to the [European] Community on efficiency grounds.

Two economic criteria can be used as necessary conditions for assigning on efficiency grounds a particular policy function to the Community:

(i) assignment of a policy function at the national level is inefficient because of the existence of cross-country spill-overs giving rise to externalities; since national governments do not take fully into account the consequences of their actions on the rest of the Community, they are bound to take suboptimal decisions;

(ii) the management of a policy function involves indivisibilities and/or economies of scale, which imply that productivity and effectiveness are improved when it is performed at a higher level.

For both criteria it is essential that externalities or economies of scale are significant at the Community level. Environmental effects (e.g. acid rain) provide classic cases of externalities; other examples can also be found in macroeconomic policy. Community-wide economies of scale are apparent in certain R&D investments (e.g. space programmes).

For the assignment to the Community level to be an adequate response, it is however necessary that two additional conditions are met:

(a) this assignment is demonstrated to yield net benefits after administrative costs and the balance of government versus market failures are taken into account, and

(b) *ad hoc* coordination among national governments is not sufficient to correct for inefficiencies.

Other motives of assignment of tasks to the Community level can stem from distributional or citizenship considerations.

Source: Quoted verbatim from Commission of the European Communities, Directorate General for Economic and Financial Affairs, "One Market, One Money," *European Economy* 44 (October 1990): 33.

Europeans have substantially researched and even "blueprinted" many critical aspects of the creation of an economic and monetary union.[4]

---

4 See, for example, Commission of the European Communities, Directorate General for Economic and Financial Affairs, "One Market, One Money," *European Economy* 44 (October 1990).

Outline of the Study

More formally, Chapter 2 serves as backdrop to the analysis. In order to understand just what is involved in "reconstituting" an economic union in a "post-Canada" scenario, it is important to recognize the various ways and means by which Canada's existing economic union is constituted. This is the first of the background sections of Chapter 2. The second focuses on selected interprovincial trade flows, to lend perspective on the nature of the potential distribution of losses across the provinces if the economic union fragments.

The next three chapters assume a separation between Quebec and ROC, and direct attention to the process and substance of reconstituting a CQEMU. Chapter 3 begins this by focusing on securing the economic-union aspects of a CQEMU. Accordingly, it deals in turn with common tariff and commercial policies, with asset and liability sharing, with framing a free trade agreement between Quebec and the United States and, finally, with reconstituting the economic union.

Chapter 4 then focuses on securing the monetary union component of a CQEMU. Attention is directed in turn to the stabilization aspects — the EuroFed or "CanaFed" and the associated deficit constraints — and to the adjustment aspects. In terms of structure, the first part of the chapter reproduces European experience and proposals. The analysis then turns to similar challenges for a Quebec-ROC monetary union.

Is a CQEMU feasible? Is it desirable? This assessment, which looks at administrative, political, and economic criteria, constitutes Chapter 5.

The conclusion that emerges from all of this is that a CQEMU is probably not in the cards. This being so, alternative scenarios must be addressed. Chapter 6 deals with the implications, for Quebec, of independence *without* a CQEMU; Chapter 7 repeats this scenario, but shifts the focus to ROC.

The concluding chapter deals with alternative approaches to maintaining Canada's political integrity. In terms of the flow of the analysis, this focus on reconstituted federalism may appear to be more of a fallback or cost-minimization scenario. However, the chapter treats renewed federalism as a first-best and positive-sum scenario. Indeed, it represents the opening salvo in the "new" constitutional debate — namely, how to redesign Canada institutionally and economically to ensure that Canadians regain their former status in the pecking order of global competitiveness.[5]

I now begin the analysis by focusing on the multitude of ways in which Canada secures its existing economic union.

---

5 As noted earlier, a full development of the various aspects of this emerging "constitutional opportunity" is beyond the scope of this study.

Chapter 2

Characteristics of Canada's Current Economic Union

Securing the Existing Economic Union

To continue with the European Community (EC) model for "post-Canada", it should be remembered that the EC is first and foremost an economic union. The Treaty of Rome, which came into force for the original six members on January 11, 1958, provided the important first tier of the economic union — essentially a common market with a common external tariff. "Europe 1992" completes this transition toward a single European market.[1]

It should not be surprising to find that, as of January 1, 1993 — and even earlier, for that matter — certain aspects of the free flow of goods, services, labor, and capital in Europe will be less impeded than corresponding flows in Canada or the United States. This is so because federations are underpinned by political blueprints — that is, constitutions — rather than by economic blueprints, and impediments such as preferential provincial or state purchasing typically are not covered by these political or constitutional blueprints. And where they are covered, their adherence is generally filtered

---

1 As Daniel Soberman points out, "Europe 1992" is underpinned by two related initiatives: the EC White Paper "Completing the Internal Market," issued in June 1985, and the resulting creation in 1986 of a *Single European Act* to amend and consolidate the various separate treaties covering coal and steel, atomic energy, and general economic arrangements. See Daniel Soberman, "European Integration: Are There Lessons for Canada?" in Ronald L. Watts and Douglas M. Brown, eds., *Options for a New Canada* (Toronto: University of Toronto Press, 1991), pp. 191–206.

through the political process, not through the administrative or legal processes that characterize economic unions.

At this juncture, it is instructive to recall that one of the messages of the "Pink Paper" released by the Canadian federal government during the constitutional debate of 1980–82 was that the "economic union" provisions in some other federations, such as the United States, were more thoroughgoing than those in Canada.[2] For example, the U.S. courts have given a much broader sweep to the "interstate commerce clause" than courts in this country have given to the Canadian Constitution's "trade and commerce power".[3] Whether this will remain the case now that the Canada-U.S. Free Trade Agreement (FTA) is in place is open to speculation. My view is that the Canadian courts *will* place much more emphasis on this clause, particularly in striking down internal market barriers. The underlying point, however, is that even federations like the United States, with quite thoroughgoing economic union or internal market provisions, have not been able to ride herd over such impediments as state purchasing preferences. Nor are they ever likely to be able to remove all internal barriers, since, almost inevitably, economic union issues are inexorably intertwined with the underlying political dimensions of federalism.

Notwithstanding these caveats, it is mischievous and even misleading to downplay Canada's accomplishments on the internal economic union front — accomplishments which the Treaty of Rome plus the nearly 300 directives of "Europe 1992" will never fully parallel, in my view, particularly in the area of labor mobility.[4] In

---

2 Jean Chrétien, *Securing the Canadian Economic Union in the Constitution* (Ottawa: Supply and Services Canada, 1980).

3 Section 91, paragraph 2 of the Constitution.

4 This does not imply that Canadians can be complacent on this issue. For example, the recent initiatives of the premiers to design a set of principles to enhance aspects of the Canadian economic union are a welcome step. As another example, but at the federal-provincial level, it is surely time to make occupational pensions fully portable, perhaps through "third-party" repositories for pensions. Moreover, the Canadian Manufacturers' Association has identified well over $5 billion of contracts that are "protected" by the various impediments to Canada's internal economic union. And so on.

order to comprehend what reconstituting an economic union would entail, it is useful to highlight just a few of what must be literally thousands of provisions, programs, laws, codes of conduct, and so on that constitute the existing Canadian internal economic union:

- First, of course, is the Constitution itself. Reference has already been made to the trade and commerce power. Section 121 — "All articles of the growth, produce or manufacture of any one of the Provinces shall, from and after the Union, be admitted free into each of the other Provinces" — guarantees, in effect, a version of a customs union, although in the context of the constitutional discussions that took place in 1980–82, several analysts recommended that this clause be amended to include services explicitly.
- Second, and related, the standardization of weights, measures, and the like, as well as a single federal agency to evaluate and eventually to lend Canada's imprimatur to new drugs, for example, seem so obvious that Canadians never even think of this area as critical in terms of promoting internal mobility of goods and services.
- Third, the presence of a single currency adds enormously to the efficiency of an economic union. Estimates for the European economic and monetary union (EEMU) indicate that a single currency for Europe can generate transaction-cost efficiencies of about 0.4 percent of the Community's GDP, with the gains for the smaller countries probably in the range of 1 percent.[5] And the potential gains go well beyond those related directly to currency conversion. A related point is that the manner in which the Canadian banking system is organized also enhances the economic union — particularly if the comparison is with the U.S. banking system.

---

5 Commission of the European Communities, Directorate General for Economic and Financial Affairs, "One Market, One Money," *European Economy* 44 (October 1990), chap. 3.

- Fourth, since 1982 the Canadian Charter of Rights and Freedoms has clearly enhanced the mobility and economic opportunities of all Canadians.
- Fifth, Canada's internal economic union is enhanced by many interprovincial agreements. For example, despite the absence of any federal role, the provinces and their respective securities commissions have created an effective national securities market.
- Sixth, federal-provincial pacts also play a critical role. Consider income taxation, for example. On the personal income tax (PIT) side, membership in the Tax Collection Agreements explicitly requires a commitment on the part of the provinces to maintain the integrity of the economic union. Indeed, setting Quebec aside — which has its own separate PIT — the Canadian PIT system is frequently viewed in comparative federalism circles as an ideal model for a federal nation: harmonized yet decentralized. On the corporate tax side, all provinces have agreed to a formula that allocates taxable income across provinces, thereby ensuring neither double nor zero taxation of corporate income — again unlike the situation in the United States.
- Seventh, the use of the federal spending power effectively converts provincial programs in the areas of health and welfare into national programs.
- Eighth, and similarly, the existence of national programs like unemployment insurance (UI) and the Canada Pension Plan and Quebec Pension Plan enhance mobility. (Or, at least, they have the *potential* to do so. The fact that UI may in practice frustrate mobility in some areas relates to errors in policy design, not to the principle underlying the program).
- Finally — although, as emphasized earlier, certainly not exhaustively — the right of citizenship conveys implicit if not explicit access to all things "Canadian".

To be sure, the very nature of a federation ensures that these internal market provisions are sometimes filtered through the political process, in the same way that the rights and freedoms under the Charter are "subject...to such reasonable limits...as can be demonstrably justified in a free and democratic society." By contrast, the internal market provisions in an economic union (such as the EC), as distinct from a political union, inevitably tend to be filtered through the legal and administrative process. One consequence of this is that, for selected areas, economic unions like the EC appear to deliver more thoroughgoing internal markets and indeed may do so.

One final perspective on Canada's economic union merits attention. As noted above, there is considerable room for improving the free flow of goods, services, and factors across the country. The automatic reaction on the part of most Canadians is that all that is really needed here to enhance the economic union is to "bring the provinces into line". This is surely part of the answer, since the provinces do mount most of the high-profile barriers to the internal market. But it is probably not the most important part.

To see this, it is important to recognize that a barrier to the economic union includes any initiative that alters the wage/rental rate or the labor/leisure choice or the tax price of public goods on a geographical basis. From this perspective, the federal government is a very major player — regional development policies, regionally differentiated UI, transportation subsidies, external commercial policy that bites differently across regions, equalization (or at least "overequalization"), and surely the now-defunct National Energy Program are all examples of the key role Ottawa plays. Note also that some of the high-profile provincial barriers — such as marketing boards and trucking restrictions — exist only because the federal government has enacted enabling legislation for provincial initiatives. Nearly a decade ago, John Whalley concluded that these "federal" impediments dominated provincial barriers in terms of their implications for GNP.[6]

Two implications derive from this. First, many Canadians would not want a full-blown internal economic union if this meant that *all* players were made to toe the line. In other words, while a thorough-

---

6 John Whalley, "Induced Distortions of Interprovincial Activity: An Overview of Issues," in Michael J. Trebilcock et al., eds., *Federalism and the Canadian Economic Union* (Toronto: Ontario Economic Council, 1983), pp. 161–200.

going economic union presumably would serve to maximize national GNP, it might not maximize Canadians' *welfare*.[7] While Canadians frequently view "Europe 1992" as an approach to be imitated, they tend to overlook the fact that an incredible internal market distortion — the Common Agricultural Policy — continues unabated.

The second implication is that, from this broader perspective, the provinces are not the villains that they are frequently made out to be. Or, if they are, then Ottawa must be as well.

The obvious next question is: How important is the internal market? Or, in terms of the thrust of this study, are internal trade flows such that it is in all provinces' interests to opt for a Canada-Quebec economic and monetary union (CQEMU) if this country's political integrity is rent asunder? To this I now turn.

Interprovincial Trade Flows

Given that the goal of much of this study is to assess the viability of a CQEMU, the next logical order of business is to attempt to quantify the role that interprovincial trade plays across Canada. Toward this end, Table 1 presents comparable data for 1974 and 1989 relating to manufacturing shipments for Ontario and Quebec. The first and most obvious conclusion that arises from these data is that both provinces are progressively orienting their manufacturing exports away from other provinces and toward the international economy — presumably the United States, but the breakdown of exports is not available. The second conclusion — and one that is every bit as pertinent to the ensuing analysis — is that, in terms of market share, Ontario is far more important to Quebec (14.51 percent of Quebec's 1989 shipments go to Ontario) than is Quebec to Ontario (5.87 percent of Ontario's shipments are destined for Quebec).

---

7 See James R. Melvin, "Political Structure and the Pursuit of Economic Objectives," in Trebilcock et al., eds., *Federalism and the Canadian Economic Union*, pp. 111–158.

Table 1: *Manufacturing Shipments by Ontario and Quebec, 1974 and 1989*

	Value of Shipments	Distribution to:			
		Quebec	Ontario	Other Provinces	Abroad
	(current $ billions)	*(percentage share)*			
Ontario					
1974					
All manufacturing	40.6	11.45	51.31	16.51	20.73
Food & beverages	5.9	10.42	69.21	15.28	5.09
Clothing	0.4	14.53	50.77	33.50	1.20
Paper & allied products	2.4	11.94	53.86	6.52	27.68
Transportation equipment	7.8	6.37	25.25	9.67	59.71
1989					
All manufacturing	166.3	5.87	46.63	13.22	34.28
Food & beverages	18.1	9.41	64.75	20.37	5.47
Clothing	2.0	13.32	53.16	31.02	2.50
Paper & allied products	7.7	10.53	42.29	12.54	34.64
Transportation equipment	44.0	1.79	12.89	2.56	82.76
Quebec					
1974					
All manufacturing	22.6	49.11	19.17	18.13	13.59
Food & beverages	3.9	70.96	12.29	12.20	4.55
Clothing	1.4	41.05	22.75	32.51	3.69
Paper & allied products	2.4	39.32	18.67	6.62	35.39
Transportation equipment	1.4	19.84	11.33	23.45	45.38
1989					
All manufacturing	80.7	49.22	14.51	10.33	25.94
Food & beverages	10.8	74.04	10.31	7.41	8.24
Clothing	4.3	57.26	23.89	15.61	3.24
Paper & allied products	8.1	24.69	16.78	2.55	55.98
Transportation equipment	7.5	20.77	8.82	4.85	65.56

Source: 1974 data are from Statistics Canada; 1989 data are preliminary estimates, from Arthur Donner, "Interprovincial Economic Links Getting Weaker," *Toronto Star*, February 18, 1991, pp. C1, C2.

In more detail, 37.3 percent of Quebec's shipments in 1974 went to ROC (with roughly one-half of these going to Ontario). By 1989, this had declined to 24.84 percent, but with Ontario's share (14.51 percent) falling much less than Quebec's exports to the other provinces. By contrast, international exports rose from 13.59 percent of total shipments in 1974 to 25.94 percent, or roughly double.

Ontario's patterns are broadly similar: a fall in east-west shipments from 27.96 percent in 1974 to 19.09 percent in 1989. Intriguingly, the bulk of the decline comes from shipments to Quebec, which fell from 11.45 percent to 5.87 percent. As is the case with Quebec, Ontario's international exports mushroomed over this period, from 20.73 percent to 34.28 percent.

Thus, in spite of the increasing north-south orientation evident in the table, Quebec still looks to "the Rest of Canada" (ROC) for fully one-quarter of its overall manufacturing shipments and toward Ontario for the major portion of this. In other words, Quebec's exports of manufacturing shipments are roughly equally split between ROC and international markets. Hence, for Quebec, re-establishing comprehensive trade links with ROC and with the United States is an absolute priority under any independence scenario. Presumably, the pressures for maximizing trade apply to Ontario as well.

Ontario, however, has quite different priorities. For it, the international market — in other words, the United States — is absolutely key, followed by the other eight provinces, with Quebec a distant third. While it would be the height of folly for any province to turn its back on any market, in any breakup scenario Quebec would be far more vulnerable than Ontario — a fact that would surely be reflected in any bargaining process. This is quite apart from the fact that the western provinces, particularly Alberta and British Columbia, probably will take a much harder line against Quebec than will Ontario and, as a result, may cater to aspects of Ontario's concerns within ROC as a *quid quo pro.*

There is one caveat. This analysis has been conducted in terms of *percentages* of total manufacturing shipments. In dollar terms, the Quebec-Ontario flows are more equal: Quebec exports roughly

$12 billion of manufacturing shipments to Ontario, while Ontario responds with roughly $10 billion.[8]

An advantage of the data in Table 1 is that they relate to 1989. The weakness is that they focus only on Quebec and Ontario and then only on manufacturing shipments. To provide a more comprehensive overview of interprovincial trade, one has to focus on 1984 data — which are still not fully adequate because they do not take account of services trade or the flow of people.[9] Table 2 presents exports of goods, classified as primary, manufacturing, and others, from each province to every other province. The table is self-explanatory and the task of sorting out the cross-province flows will basically be left to the reader. However, it is useful to highlight a few points.[10]

Most provinces undertake a great deal of trade with other Canadian provinces. Indeed, Quebec, Prince Edward Island, Nova Scotia, Manitoba, Saskatchewan, and Alberta rely more heavily on domestic trade than on international trade. In all cases, trade with other countries is also important. Ontario, Newfoundland, New Brunswick, and British Columbia rely more heavily on international trade than domestic trade. Among the three largest manufacturing provinces (Ontario, Quebec, and British Columbia), only Quebec is

---

8 There is another caveat, which will be detailed later: much of Ontario's international exports are automobile related. Were Quebec to separate, this auto trade might be in considerable jeopardy, since Ontario would no longer be able to "deliver" the Quebec market.

9 For one of the most extensive treatments of these 1984 interprovincial and international trade flows by province, see Pierre-Paul Proulx, "Un examin des échanges commerciaux du Québec avec les autres provinces canadiennes, les États-Unis et le reste du monde," in Quebec, Commission on the Political and Constitutional Future of Quebec [Bélanger-Campeau Commission], *Éléments d'analyse économique pertinents à la révision du statut politique et constitutionnel du Québec* [Background papers], vol.1 (Quebec, 1991). The interested reader may wish to consult this source. Rather than attempting to summarize Proulx, I have opted to present a federal Department of Finance summary of these 1984 data in a single table (Table 2).

10 These are largely paraphrased from "Economic Linkages among Provinces," *Quarterly Economic Review* (Canada, Department of Finance), March 1991, pp. 34–54.

more dependent on trade with other provinces than on international markets. For Ontario and British Columbia, exports to other provinces account for 35.5 and 28 percent, respectively, of total out-of-province shipments and 17 and 13.5 percent, respectively, of total shipments — that is, out-of-province shipments and shipments remaining within the originating province. A final set of comments relating to Table 2 is relevant.

- First, Ontario is the largest provincial market for seven of the nine other provinces. Quebec is the largest customer for New Brunswick, while Alberta holds this position for exports of B.C. goods. In both of these cases, Ontario is the second-largest customer.
- Second, the largest provincial export percentage in the entire table is that for Quebec shipments of goods to Ontario — 28.78 percent.
- Third, Quebec's exports to the four western provinces amount to roughly 15 percent of its total "exports", nearly as large as the 16.5 percent figure for Ontario's percentage exports to the west.
- Fourth, except for British Columbia, the western provinces also export significant amounts to Quebec: Manitoba (8.85 percent), Saskatchewan (10.61 percent), and Alberta (10.25 percent). Only 2.28 percent of British Columbia's exports go to Quebec, but that province and Newfoundland are clear outliers, with fully 75 percent of their exports going offshore. This last point relating to the importance of Quebec as a provincial market also applies to the eastern provinces, with their exports to Quebec ranging from a low of 7.36 percent for Newfoundland to a high of 16.98 percent for New Brunswick.

None of this should be particularly surprising: the "center" represents an important export market for both east and west. What is as yet unknown is not whether, but rather by how much, the FTA will alter all of this. The evidence from Table 1 is that, from 1984 to 1989 (essentially pre-FTA), there was a dramatic shift toward north-

Table 2: **Exports of Goods by Destination, Selected Aggregates, 1984**

(as a percentage of total exports)

Destination:	Nfld.	P.E.I.	N.S.	N.B.	Que.	Ont.	Man.	Sask.	Alta.	B.C.	Total Prov.	Total Foreign
Originating province: Newfoundland												
Goods	—	0.27	4.49	0.79	7.36	11.07	0.02	0.03	0.07	0.10	24.22	75.78
Primary	—	0.00	3.65	0.32	0.05	15.31	0.00	0.00	0.00	0.00	19.34	80.66
Manufacturing	—	0.54	5.81	1.32	3.24	8.47	0.04	0.07	0.14	0.20	19.88	80.12
Other	—	0.00	0.00	0.00	98.42	0.00	0.00	0.00	0.00	0.00	98.42	1.58
Originating Province: Prince Edward Island												
Goods	5.67	—	11.13	7.87	9.31	21.33	0.35	0.09	0.33	0.23	56.56	43.44
Primary	3.31	—	8.60	9.30	10.06	26.80	0.58	0.00	0.06	0.00	58.55	41.45
Manufacturing	7.25	—	12.83	6.90	8.81	17.67	0.19	0.16	0.51	0.39	55.23	44.77
Other	0.00	—	0.00	0.00	0.00	0.00	0.00	0.00	0.00	0.00	0.00	0.00
Originating Province: Nova Scotia												
Goods	7.56	3.04	—	12.95	14.49	20.08	0.79	0.47	1.41	1.10	61.99	38.01
Primary	5.54	0.91	—	6.79	2.03	60.23	0.00	0.00	0.00	0.00	75.56	24.44
Manufacturing	8.15	3.62	—	13.85	17.87	9.77	1.00	0.59	1.79	1.40	58.18	41.82
Other	0.00	0.00	—	90.94	0.00	0.00	0.00	0.00	0.00	0.00	90.94	9.06
Originating Province: New Brunswick												
Goods	2.99	3.32	9.36	—	16.98	11.52	0.46	0.39	0.86	0.62	46.60	53.40
Primary	0.16	1.28	4.60	—	23.25	3.27	0.00	0.00	0.00	0.00	32.57	67.43
Manufacturing	3.99	3.37	11.50	—	18.01	14.81	0.62	0.52	1.16	0.84	54.93	45.07
Other	0.00	6.06	0.98	—	0.10	0.00	0.00	0.00	0.00	0.00	7.17	92.83
Originating Province: Quebec												
Goods	2.61	0.45	2.86	3.34	—	28.78	1.81	2.67	5.87	4.57	53.66	46.34
Primary	3.60	0.21	1.56	2.26	—	28.99	0.00	0.00	0.03	0.00	42.64	57.36
Manufacturing	2.60	0.47	3.00	3.12	—	28.89	1.96	2.88	6.34	4.93	54.58	45.42
Other	0.19	0.00	0.00	18.09	—	22.48	0.00	0.00	0.00	0.00	40.75	59.25

Table 2 - continued

Destination:	Nfld.	P.E.I.	N.S.	N.B.	Que.	Ont.	Man.	Sask.	Alta.	B.C.	Total Prov.	Total Foreign
Originating Province: Ontario												
Goods	1.26	0.30	2.14	1.54	14.94	—	2.87	2.35	6.58	4.69	37.10	62.90
Primary	0.23	0.34	2.80	0.52	33.90	—	3.20	1.26	0.67	0.53	43.45	56.55
Manufacturing	1.32	0.30	2.11	1.61	14.03	—	2.87	2.43	6.94	4.94	36.99	63.01
Other	0.02	0.02	0.00	0.02	0.04	—	0.00	0.00	0.00	0.02	0.11	99.89
Originating Province: Manitoba												
Goods	0.65	0.06	0.75	0.66	8.85	23.81	—	8.75	10.15	4.27	58.41	41.59
Primary	0.03	0.01	0.17	0.14	11.92	34.04	—	1.38	7.00	1.44	56.14	43.86
Manufacturing	0.93	0.08	1.01	0.89	7.55	18.75	—	12.01	11.63	5.57	59.10	40.90
Other	0.00	0.00	0.00	0.00	0.00	87.04	—	12.96	0.00	0.00	100.00	0.00
Originating Province: Saskatchewan												
Goods	0.01	0.01	0.20	0.13	10.61	12.62	4.96	—	5.32	1.24	35.31	64.69
Primary	0.02	0.01	0.16	0.12	11.19	12.21	2.78	—	3.51	0.56	30.58	69.42
Manufacturing	0.00	0.00	0.29	0.16	9.40	13.08	9.51	—	9.55	2.87	45.54	54.46
Other	0.00	0.00	0.00	0.00	0.00	42.15	43.05	—	11.88	0.00	97.09	2.91
Originating Province: Alberta												
Goods	0.06	0.02	0.21	1.39	10.25	26.26	3.74	6.55	—	9.95	59.62	40.38
Primary	0.00	0.01	0.17	1.99	12.81	33.50	0.76	3.82	—	7.45	60.88	39.12
Manufacturing	0.17	0.05	0.28	0.22	5.07	12.04	9.57	11.94	—	14.89	56.97	43.03
Other	0.00	0.00	0.00	0.00	49.67	34.59	10.64	0.00	—	0.00	100.00	0.00
Originating Province: British Columbia												
Goods	0.12	0.06	0.21	0.25	2.28	6.80	1.19	2.24	10.09	—	24.87	75.13
Primary	0.01	0.01	0.02	0.00	1.17	14.08	0.37	1.84	7.14	—	26.34	73.66
Manufacturing	0.15	0.08	0.27	0.32	2.63	4.87	1.45	2.39	9.78	—	23.57	76.43
Other	0.00	0.00	0.00	0.00	0.00	0.00	0.00	0.00	76.18	—	76.18	23.82

Source: Canada, Department of Finance, *Quarterly Economic Review* (March 1991), Table 11.A4.

south and away from east-west trade. East-west trade remains vitally important, however, and all provinces would be clearly worse off if these trade flows were interrupted.

To conclude this section, I repeat the earlier observation that, in terms of the "center", maintaining free trade, and, indeed, striving for an economic union is more of a priority for Quebec than it is for Ontario, although it remains essential for the economic viability of both provinces.

With these interprovincial trade flows and the existing provisions for securing the Canadian economic union as backdrop, I now turn to the nature and substance of the arrangements that must be put in place to "recreate" a CQEMU once Canada's political integrity is rent.

Chapter 3

Securing the Economic Union Component of a CQEMU

In Chapter 2, the point was made that, if and when Quebec declares itself independent and, therefore, outside the Canadian political and legal framework, the existing economic union between Quebec and "the Rest of Canada" (ROC) would be similarly dissolved. The focus of this and the following two chapters is on the nature and substance of the new arrangements that would have to be put in place to "recreate" a Canada-Quebec economic and monetary union (CQEMU).

Common Tariff and Commercial Policies

Free trade arrangements such as the European Free Trade Association and the Canada-U.S. Free Trade Agreement (FTA) typically do not require common external commercial policies and tariffs. Rather, they generally require "rules of origin" or "domestic-value-added" provisions in order that third countries do not use preferential access to one member nation to "export" to other member nations of the free trade arrangements. Likewise, common currency areas need not have common external commercial policies — the operations of the gold standard come to mind here.

Almost by definition, however, economic unions *do* require common external policies. This is so because, under a reconstituted, full-blown economic union, there would be no impediments to exporting goods or services from Quebec to ROC (or vice versa), regardless of the ultimate origin of these goods and services. Thus, one of the initial issues to be settled in any economic union between a sovereign Quebec and a sovereign ROC is the nature of the common external policy.

It is probably the case that the status quo with respect to tariffs, quotas, and other aspects of external commercial policy would have a much better chance of surviving intact if the movement toward sovereignty and an economic union were to proceed *without* an initial rending of Canada's political and legal framework. This is so because embedded in this country's external commercial policy are literally decades of delicate regional and sectoral tradeoffs. Once these existing compromises are rendered extra-legal — through, for example, an early unilateral declaration of independence on the part of Quebec — everything is up for grabs.[1] Why would British Columbia, say, agree to a reconstituted commercial policy that implicitly, if not explicitly, subsidizes Quebec textile workers and furniture manufacturers? On an even higher-profile issue, why would any of the other provinces agree to Quebec's dairy farmers continuing to get a 60 percent share of industrial milk production quotas? At best, they would get their population share. And this is not merely an issue between Quebec and ROC. Why should British Columbia cater to central Canadian (primarily Ontario) auto workers if this means Toyotas will cost more in Vancouver? Or, to put it differently, what would British Columbia ask for in return?

The point is not to argue that this exercise would be impossible. Clearly, it would not be, as the European Community (EC) has demonstrated: the Treaty of Rome embodied a common external tariff. The European situation was, however, entirely different. The initial six members of the EC were engaging in a positive-sum game involving both trade creation and trade diversion, the latter helped along by a significant "Fortress Europe" external tariff. Quebec and ROC probably would be involved in a negative-sum game — at least

---

1 As Richard Harris has pointed out in "Post-Meech Economics: Some Observations" (Department of Economics, Simon Fraser University, Burnaby, B.C., 1990, mimeographed).

over some considerable period of time — that likely would be magnified because the existing degree of trade diversion might get swept away in common tariff negotiations. What the Europeans are also demonstrating is that the move from a customs union (1958) to a single market (1992) to a common currency (mid-1990s at the earliest) is an arduous, brick-by-brick building process. The assumption implicit in much of the "association" discussion, particularly within Quebec, is that since we are "already there", as it were, the process of dismantling and reconstruction should be able to proceed much more easily and quickly. This section suggests that negotiations relating to re-establishing a common commercial policy would be complex, difficult, and, if the breakup is acrimonious, punitive on both sides. Even more problematical would be the division of assets and liabilities, to which I now turn.

Debt and Asset Sharing

In an important sense, the division of debt and assets would be the single most critical issue in terms of the prospects for a CQEMU. If both sides are satisfied that the division has been "fair", then this may establish a climate conducive to the remainder of the negotiations toward a full-blown CQEMU, including the reconstituting of a common external commercial policy.

Although debt and asset sharing will play a key role in the discussions on Canada's constitutional future, space does not permit me to tackle this subject here with any degree of appropriate detail.[2] Instead, my approach is to inject it where relevant into the ensuing analysis. For example, the allocation of the federal debt will loom large when it comes to the viability of a common Quebec-ROC

---

2 This is not a serious a problem, however, since debt sharing has already attracted substantial attention. See, for example, Paul Boothe and Richard Harris, "Alternative Divisions of Federal Assets and Liabilities" (Paper presented to a conference on "Economic Dimensions of Constitutional Change," Kingston, Ont., John Deutsch Institute for the Study of Economic Policy, Queen's University, June 4–6, 1991).

currency, and the implications will be elaborated in this later context. Nonetheless, some initial observations are in order.

Both the Parti Québécois and the Allaire Report accepted that an independent Quebec would be responsible for its "fair share" of the net debt. This acceptance has been generally assumed — in both Quebec and ROC — to imply that negotiations would focus on whether the appropriate share for Quebec would be its proportion of the population (roughly 25 percent) or the somewhat lower share that would arise from using the province's share of Canada's gross domestic product (GDP) as the allocating mechanism. In this context, the claim in the background studies to the Bélanger-Campeau Report that Quebec's appropriate share is 18.5 percent caught most observers by surprise — and obviously some by delight as well![3] The argument is based on the proposition that since an independent Quebec would acquire 18.5 percent of existing federal assets, this is the proportion of the debt it should assume. To bolster this position, the Commission Secretariat (which was the author of Chapter 9) drew on the advice of two international authorities whose pronouncements included the following three propositions:[4]

- the negotiations of Quebec secession would be in the framework of international law as well as Canadian law;
- the Commission's approach to asset and debt division — namely, equating asset and liability shares — violates no established international norm; and
- international precedent leans toward favoring the "successor state" (Quebec) rather than the predecessor state (Canada).

---

3 Quebec, Commission on the Political and Constitutional Future of Quebec, *Report* (Quebec, March 27, 1991), chap. 9.

4 The two experts are Professor Malcolm Shaw, Faculty of Law, University of Leicester, and Geneviève Burdeau, Faculty of Law, University of Dijon. Their advice appears in Annex B.2 and Annex B.4, respectively, appended to Chapter 9 of volume I of the background studies to the Bélanger-Campeau Commission. See also Robert Mackenzie, "The Nation: Sovereignists Did Their Homework," *Toronto Star*, April 13, 1991, p. D4.

Needless to say, some quite significant implications attend these pronouncements.

First, setting aside whether or not the calculation of Quebec's share of assets is conducted appropriately, ROC would never accept a net debt allocation based on this principle, since, among other things, it neglects entirely the workings of the tax-transfer (for example, equalization) and interprovincial redistribution (for example, unemployment insurance) systems that ROC perceives to have worked massively in Quebec's favor over the years. The fallacy of the Bélanger-Campeau Secretariat's approach is as follows: deficits feed directly into debt, but not into assets, since, apart from physical assets, deficits have been used to finance human capital formation — which are not included in the Secretariat's calculations — and, most importantly, consumption. It is very difficult to make the case that Quebecers have not come off rather well in terms of federal largesse. Ultimately, then, the distributional mechanism likely would come down to population or, if Quebec is lucky and the discussions are harmonious, perhaps GDP share.

Quebec's failure to assume what ROC perceives as an "appropriate" share of the common debt burden — regardless of what international precedence may be — would surely trigger an acrimonious breakup that would carry over to *all* other aspects of a CQEMU, including the re-establishment of a common commercial policy. This is all the more the case, since, as was shown earlier, Quebec is more trade dependent on ROC than ROC is on Quebec, and the mood in ROC is now tilting in the direction of digging in heels and levering off any ROC advantage, perceived or real.

The second implication is that Quebec may draw some significant advantage from the fact that ROC assumes — indeed, desires — that "Canada" will continue to exist. What this means is that any breakup would of necessity fall into the successor-state/ predecessor-state framework alluded to above. Apart from the fact that this might be wishful thinking — that is, there is no guarantee that ROC would continue to exist as a single political entity — it surely does transfer some advantage to Quebec. In terms of the external debt, for example, this implies that *all* existing bonds would remain the liability of ROC.

Indeed, as long as "Canada" is the "predecessor" state, Quebec could not "legally" assume a portion of the Canadian debt. Thus, what sharing the existing debt effectively would mean under this scenario is that Quebec would undertake a series of side payments to ROC to cover its annual "share" of debt servicing and any debt retirements. Should Quebec renege on these side payments, it is "Canada's" or ROC's credit rating as much as Quebec's that would be hit. How would ROC inform a U.S. insurance company that it should henceforth collect 25 percent (or 18.5 percent) of interest owing from Quebec and the remainder from ROC? It could not.

Moreover, even if one could envisage some divvying up of the existing debt on a once-and-for-all basis, this would not get ROC out of the bind. Should Quebec default on its portion, in whole or even in part, the above-mentioned insurance company would surely view this capital loss or capital "expropriation" as a result of having bought Canadian bonds in the first place. With sources of net capital drying up all over the world — as Japan repatriates and as Germany and the Middle East shift from being suppliers to being demanders — "see you!" increasingly would be the message to Quebec and ROC alike.

To be sure, this is a dismal scenario. But aspects of it would surely be triggered if and when the international capital markets assess the potential risks of finding themselves "holding the bag" in any negotiations related to whether Quebec should assume 18.5 percent or 25 percent of Canada's debt. Intriguingly, the Reform Party's Preston Manning always refers to "New Canada". Perhaps he and his party have twigged to the fact that there are costs to assuming the full legal, political, and, (where possible) constitutional continuance of "Canada". "New Canada" obviously would not be costless in credit-rating terms, but it would serve to remove the "hammer" from Quebec in any negotiations on debt and assets.

The third implication focuses on the other side of this coin. Suppose ROC and Quebec come to an amicable agreement on the division of debt and assets. Suppose further that the debt continues to be denominated in Canadian dollars and that Quebec agrees to make annual payments to ROC for its agreed-on burden sharing. Does such an arrangement not also imply that Quebec must have some say in how ROC conducts overall monetary and fiscal policy, since this clearly would have an impact on the value of the contractual arrangement into which Quebec has entered? I think the answer has to be yes, although a series of side arrangements with escape clauses might be an alternative way out.

The issue here is that Quebec ought to receive some assurance that ROC would not attempt to monetize the deficit, driving interest rates and debt servicing sky high. Consider the opposite vantage point. Would ROC accept a 25 percent allocation of the debt to Quebec, but denominated in a new Quebec currency, which Quebec could devalue by, say, 10 percent ten minutes after the agreement, thereby not only gaining an export edge into ROC but also "reneging" on its debt sharing (in Canadian dollars) by 10 percent? Surely not. Thus, the commonly articulated ROC position that (a) Quebec accept its "fair" share of the debt burden denominated in Canadian dollars but that (b) Quebec will have no say in ROC's macro affairs — that is, on what happens to the Canadian dollar — is, I think, a total nonstarter. It is precisely in this area that international law and the "preference" for successor states might come into play.

Thus, while the issue of the debt overhang and the options for its allocation between Quebec and ROC are incredibly complex in their own right, they also have very significant implications for virtually all other aspects of "post-Canada", whether or not the outcome is a CQEMU or independent states. As an important aside, the assumption underlying the above discussion has been that it is Quebec, not ROC, that would be under pressure in terms of digesting its share of the debt. This is not obvious given, on the one hand, that Quebec has been preparing its public and private finances for this eventuality for more than a decade and, on the other, that ROC — in particular, Ontario, as reflected in its recent budget — has essentially refused to recognize that the status quo is rapidly losing its economic viability.

A Quebec-U.S.
Free Trade Agreement

Before focusing on the details of the economic and monetary union between Canada and Quebec, one more building block needs to be put in place. Specifically, both Quebec and ROC must secure their trading relationships with the United States. It is all too often assumed that this is a problem only for Quebec. Surely this is incorrect. If ROC — that is, in this case, Ontario — can no longer "deliver" the Quebec car market, the auto pact obviously would come under review.

Whether this would trigger the opening up of the entire Canada-U.S. FTA is an open issue. Powerful U.S. interests are ready and willing to push for new provisions — on culture, for example. In any event, *some* changes would be needed to the FTA, since it is, after all, a bilateral agreement. With Quebec also in, it would become trilateral (or multilateral), and the provisions relating to the composition of the various review panels and settlement mechanisms would have to be altered. Again, this would be an opportunity for U.S. interests to press for new demands. The point is that one cannot simply assume that present trading arrangements between the United States and the rest of Canada would remain in place if Quebec separates. And this is quite apart from the fact that the Bob Raes of ROC would, from their official statements, be quite prepared to let the FTA languish.

It seems fair to say, however, that it is Quebec that would face the much greater challenge. There are two or three potential stumbling blocks in the path of a Quebec-U.S. FTA.

The first relates to one of Quebec's inherent strengths: "Quebec Inc.", the Japanese or continental European type of relationship among government, business, financial institutions, and the Caisse de dépôt, and related aspects such as the threshold requirements — typically linked to investment in the province — needed to qualify foreign companies as "Quebec partners" and, hence, able to bid on government contracts. It is fairly obvious that this approach to industrial organization runs against that of the United States — and, indeed, the Anglo-Saxon world generally. Not quite so obvious is why the United States might insist on writing its own approach to competition policy into any new FTA. Part of the answer relates to the fact that the United States has already told Japan that it will not allow that country to "export" *keiretsu* to this side of the Pacific. If it were to accommodate Quebec by acceding to "Quebec Inc.", its bargaining power with Japan would be considerably diminished.

A second potential stumbling block relates to Hydro-Québec. In the Canada-U.S. FTA, the hydroelectric utilities were exempted, perhaps because they were provincial Crown corporations. In any Quebec-U.S. FTA, however, Hydro-Québec would become a "national" government corporation, and the fact that it would be exporting power at a rate considerably above the domestic price surely would be placed on the negotiating table. So would such concerns as the subsidy to industrial giants like Norsk-Hydro, which access Quebec power at roughly one-third the domestic price.

A third possible issue is a related one. The Mexico-U.S.-Canada discussions are sure to raise the relationship of ecology and of the environment to trade. Thus, the timing for a Quebec-U.S. FTA could not be less opportune, since it would be impossible to avoid the environmental and ecological issues surrounding James Bay II. Already, substantial citizen lobbies in the U.S. northeast are ready and anxious to press this point.

It is not evident, however, that these issues would make a Quebec-U.S. FTA highly unlikely. Some argue that the U.S. Congress is in no mood to allow another administration-delivered trade deal. Other commentators believe that the United States would offer some similar deal to Quebec because the Americans would not want to generate even more problems on their northern border. But even in this group, many argue that there is plenty of scope within the existing document for the United States to address the above concerns down the road a bit.

While one cannot know for certain what the outcome would be, it is clear that, for Quebec, the risks are not only high but they are all in the same direction.

I now want to address a Quebec-U.S. FTA from a quite different angle. For this purpose, I shall adopt Quebec's best-possible-case scenario — namely, that the United States would offer the *same* deal to Quebec as it did to Canada and, further, that Quebec would sign. The question then becomes: Would anything have changed? The answer — perhaps surprisingly — is that, for Quebec, much would have changed *vis-à-vis* both the United States and ROC.

Specifically, the net result would be quite significant in terms of Quebec's maneuverability with regard to its degree of freedom under the operations of the Canada-U.S. FTA. This arises because, in several areas, *the existing FTA does very little to constrain the operations of provincial governments*. In order to amplify on this theme, I shall focus on only one area —financial institution regulation.

Among the most important provisions of Chapter 17 (Financial Institutions) of the FTA is Article 1703, which exempts U.S. residents from limits on foreign ownership of Canadian federally chartered financial institutions. What is at stake here is the so-called 10/25 rule, which prevents any single nonresident from acquiring more than 10 percent of a financial institution's shares and prevents nonresidents in aggregate from acquiring more than 25 percent of these shares. What the exemption under the FTA means is that U.S. residents now have the same ownership rights as Canadians when it comes to federally regulated financial institutions. Presumably, according to a recent report of the Canadian Senate, this implies that Americans can buy any of the large federally chartered trust companies, loan companies, and insurance companies, subject only to the same ministerial review that would apply to Canadians.[5] The Senate report goes on to note that Chapter 17 of the FTA does *not* apply to provincially chartered financial institutions:

> Thus, the Americans could not buy the Quebec-chartered arm
> of Royal Trustco because Quebec legislation incorporates the

---

5 See Canada, Parliament, Senate, Standing Committee on Banking, Trade and Commerce, *Canada 1992: Toward a National Market in Financial Services*, Eighth Report (Ottawa, 1990), p. 22.

10/25 rule. This leads in a rather anomalous direction: if Canadians want to allow trust companies to be narrowly held and also want to ensure that they remain in Canadian hands, the "solution" would be to have them charter provincially.[6]

This may be viewed as traversing quite far afield. The critical point, however, is that under the status quo, Quebecers gain all the advantages of the FTA while their government and the governments of the other provinces are not directly bound, or at least are less bound than is Ottawa, by many of its provisions.

But were Quebec itself to sign a separate FTA, as it presumably would have to if it declared its independence, then the province ("country") *would* be bound in its full range of operations. This might turn out to be quite constraining in several areas. Continuing with the focus on the financial sector, the United States, as noted earlier, has long been concerned with the Japanese/German style integration of the financial and real sectors that Quebec also espouses ("Quebec Inc."). The province might be able to sneak this by within a Canada-U.S. FTA. It is far less likely to be able to get away with it in a separate Quebec-U.S. FTA, because it would be signing as a "country" and, hence, would be bound by the provisions of Chapter 17, for example. Moreover, Quebec would no longer be able to protect its financial institutions from U.S. takeovers. And, as recent Quebec history has revealed, ownership of Quebec-based industries is central to much of Quebec's industrial strategy. In these cases, and across many other FTA provisions, Quebec's policy maneuverability might well be reduced compared with the status quo.

There is an important related issue as well. If both a ROC-U.S. FTA and a Quebec-U.S. FTA were in place, Quebec would then be more constrained than Ontario, since the latter would still be a province. For example, since financial institution ownership rules apply only to nationally chartered institutions, they would not be binding on Ontario under the ROC-U.S. FTA, but they would apply to Quebec.

---

6 Ibid., p. 23.

While this discussion has focused for the sake of example on the implications for financial institution regulations (Chapter 17 of the FTA), this is unlikely to be the most problematical area. Consider Chapter 13, Government Procurement. For Canada, 22 governmental departments and 10 agencies are covered. So are Department of National Defence purchases of certain defined products — some 99 types of products ranging from tractors to mechanical power transmission equipment to construction machinery to pumps and compressors to electric wire and power and distribution equipment. But these bind *only* at the national level. If Quebec were to sign a separate FTA with the United States, its procurement would be similarly bound — and, I would argue, Hydro-Québec would find itself included. But Ontario Hydro and the Ontario provincial government would remain exempt.

More intriguing still, would this same problem also carry over to the CQEMU? Specifically, would a CQEMU only apply at the "national" level for areas such as eliminating purchasing preferences? Or would it also bind Alberta and Ontario? If the latter, would these provinces then request direct representation, along with Quebec, in the administrative superstructure that would monitor the economic union? Under the most favorable of circumstances for Quebec, ROC would, in its own interest, secure a full-blown internal market, in which case a Quebec-Canada economic union would automatically give Quebec access to ROC's internal free market. Would this materialize? The answer is not immediately apparent. Since this is an economic union issue and since the building blocks have now been put in place in preparation for addressing the economic union, I now turn to the range of challenges related to reconstituting the ROC-Quebec economic union.

Reconstituting the Economic Union

Securing an economic union in Europe is a combination of the provisions of the Treaty of Rome plus the nearly 300 "integration directives" associated with the January 1, 1993, date for achieving the single European market. A sovereign ROC and a sovereign Quebec embarking on a CQEMU inevitably would have to replicate these or similar provisions and directives. To do so would require a legal and administrative superstructure to monitor and interpret the provisions and, when necessary, to pass binding judgment on or otherwise resolve any disputes.

The very nature of a meaningful economic union implies, however, that the sovereignty of both an independent Quebec and an independent ROC will be constrained in *all* policy areas to the extent that initiatives serve to impede the free flow of goods, services, capital, persons, and enterprises across the economic union. More to the point, the constraints on policymaking will of necessity have to be legal and administrative, not the "flexible" nature of the constraints when economic unions are run through federal systems.

In other words, while a sovereign Quebec would get control over a whole range of policy areas, the creation of an economic union with ROC would subject these new areas (and existing policy areas as well) to substantial superstructure monitoring, regulation, adjudication, and, in some areas, significant control — "Pyrrhic powers" as it were. In this context, it is instructive to refer again to the emerging European economic union — specifically to the December 10, 1990, amendments to the EC "Draft Treaty" in order to facilitate an economic and monetary union:

> Whatever fields are involved — whether competition, the opening up of public procurement, research and development, European infrastructure, labour markets, the environment, or taxation — Community policies will have to be reinforced in order to improve the general efficiency of the internal market and to increase the competitiveness of the Community economy, which is essential if the basic objectives of European Union are to be achieved.
>
> The coordination of economic policies, which is already an area for which the Community has responsibility, will have to be re-inforced....The instruments required for the conduct of economic policy will remain the prerogative of Member States.

For purposes of coordination, however, various additional instruments and procedures will have to set be up.[7]

My interpretation of the second paragraph of this quote is to
link "coordination of economic policies" — which will fall to the
Community — with the economic union principle and the "instruments" — which will remain with the national governments — with
the subsidiarity principle. One could mount an argument to the
effect that, for a CQEMU, Quebec and ROC would not let the
principle of economic union significantly erode the principle of
subsidiarity. For one thing, the national-treatment provision presumably would still prevail — Quebec would have substantial policy flexibility provided it did not discriminate against ROC firms,
and vice versa. For another, pursuing a very strict economic union
in the face of FTAs with the United States would open Quebec and
ROC to more intensive U.S. competition.

There are, however, powerful forces that would work in the
other direction. Organizations such as the Canadian Manufacturers'
Association are now complaining bitterly that there are very significant interprovincial barriers. Since the name of the game is to have
a "single market", these barriers would have to go. It seems to me
that it would be very difficult to exempt selected sectors from the
impact of the economic union.

There is a second factor that may weigh in heavily. A full-blown
economic union is potentially a highly "centralizing" concept. So,
armed with "externalities", the principle of subsidiarity might be
easy prey for an "expansive bureaucratic dynamic" at the administrative core of the economic union. Perhaps some elaboration is in
order. As indicated in the box on p. 7, the principle of subsidiarity
will give way to externalities and economies of scale as well as
environmental and macroeconomic concerns. As a concluding com-

---

7 Commission of the European Communities, "Draft Treaty Amending the Treaty
   Establishing the European Economic Community with a View to Achieving
   Economic and Monetary Union" (Brussels, December 10, 1990), pp. 8–9. The
   "additional instruments and procedures" to be set up would include economic
   policy guidelines, reinforced multilateral surveillance, and so on.

ment, the box notes that distributional and citizenship imperatives can also override the principle of subsidiarity. Armed with one or two of these riders, let alone all six, there is ample scope for the emergence of a centralist dynamic.

The third and perhaps most critical factor is that the characteristics of the economic union will be driven by the desires of ROC — or else there will be no economic union! It is not only size of market and population issues that will weigh in here, it is also the trade-flow data presented earlier — Quebec needs an economic union more than ROC does.

Setting aside for now the important issue of the structure of the confederal core of economic union, it is clear that there are substantial roadblocks to be overcome. Should a subsidy agreement be an integral part of an economic union? I think the answer has to be yes. Should government purchasing preferences be abolished? Obviously, the answer here should be yes, but problems would abound. The fact that Ottawa presumably would remain the capital of ROC would create substantial concern in, say, Nova Scotia and Alberta, since Quebec suppliers would have an obvious proximity advantage over potential suppliers from these two provinces. Should provincial governments also be subject to the elimination of preferential purchasing? Again, the answer would appear to have to be yes. However, this would also have to include the government-owned hydroelectric utilities. Should Ontario be able to import electricity from Quebec at rates identical (apart from delivery costs) to what Quebecers pay. Again, yes. All of this is really part of the expansionist bureaucratic dynamic alluded to earlier.

If one says yes to any of the above questions, it becomes very difficult not to say yes to them all. One consequence from all of this is that the provincial governments in ROC would also find their maneuverability severely constrained. This is happening in Germany, for example, where the *Länder* find that much of "Europe 1992" will constrain their existing flexibility. This is probably inevitable — the administrative and legal EC superstructure guaranteeing the European economic union will supersede the flexible political or economic union that characterizes federal Germany. If the ROC provinces likewise end up being constrained, this would add further to overall ROC demands that Quebec also be fully bound by the economic union.

Environmental Issues

Prior to concluding this chapter, it is important to direct some attention to the relationship between the environment and economic union. I would be the first to agree that current policies in this area are unsustainable. Are the environmental standards applied to the Rafferty-Alameda dam project identical to those applied to Hibernia or James Bay II? If not, these differential standards effectively become a 1990s version of a federal disallowance clause. Thus, new provisions — perhaps monitored by some impartial body at arm's length from all governments — are necessary regardless of what transpires, post-Meech. Nonetheless, it is instructive to focus on the EC's approach to environmental policy:

> Community environmental policy becomes more important in the context of the internal market for two reasons. First, it can be misused by Member States as an instrument to create new segmentation of markets in Europe. Second, allocative efficiency in economic terms becomes more and more related with ecological efficiency.[8]

In terms of the first of these reasons, "market segmentation" can occur either because "lax" standards might provide an export advantage or because some provinces in ROC, for example, could apply "import" standards with respect to the role of the environment in the production of goods, thereby mounting what could be viewed as protectionist barriers. In terms of the second reason, there appears to be growing support in Europe that ecological taxes ought to be

---

8 Commission of the European Communities, *Economic and Monetary Union* (Brussels, 1990), p. 22.

mounted at the Community level, since the externalities associated with any single nation acting alone might be very high. Although it is a bit unfair to suggest that integrating the environment and an economic union will be particularly problematical — unfair because, as noted, we have not yet sorted it out within Canada — it seems inevitable that some sort of "environmental contract" would have to underpin any ROC-Quebec economic union; on the surface at least, this would be very constraining to Quebec, since James Bay II would be front and center.

The Economic Union Component: Conclusion

Even though the impact of an economic union that is run through an administrative and legal superstructure can effectively erode national powers, the administrative cost of this "centralization" is not particularly high. For example, total EC spending is under 1.5 percent of the Community's GNP, with more than half of this allocated to the Common Agricultural Policy. Moreover, when the EC looks toward the millennium it does so in terms of numbers like just over 2 percent of GNP — and this includes some initiatives to be dealt with later under the monetary union component of a European economic and monetary union (EEMU). This is surely intriguing in light of the desire on the part of many Canadians for a strong central government, which is generally assumed also to imply a "large" central government. As my colleague Peter Leslie has observed, the EEMU is "centralizing without federalizing" — that is, without accruing major spending powers run through a popularly elected Community parliament.[9] Rather, the European administrative superstructure bites largely in terms of *how* member states can exercise their spending powers.

Discussion of the governance of the economic union and, more importantly, of its underlying feasibility and desirability will be left

---

9 See Peter Leslie, "Options for the Future of Canada: The Good, the Bad and the Fantastic," in Ronald L. Watts and Douglas M. Brown, eds., *Options for a New Canada* (Toronto: University of Toronto Press, 1990), pp. 123–140.

until the monetary union aspects of a CQEMU are addressed in the next chapter. To conclude this present chapter, the principal implication that derives from the above analysis is the one raised in the introduction: Why would Quebec risk its economic future by becoming independent only to immediately hand back to the confederal superstructure much of — and in some areas more than — the "sovereignty" that it gained?

Chapter 4

Securing the Monetary Union Component of a CQEMU

Issues surrounding the monetary union component of a European economic and monetary union (EEMU) are probably more controversial than the economic union or single market aspects. In addition, they are far more speculative, since the move toward the proposed European central bank, or "EuroFed", is still some way off, if it comes into being at all. Nonetheless, in what follows I shall devote some time to current European thinking with respect, first, to the stabilization impacts of the proposed monetary union and, second, to the adjustment or redistributional aspects. This is then followed by an assessment of (i) whether there are any lessons here for a Canada-Quebec economic and monetary union (CQEMU) and (ii) the various alternative approaches open to Quebec and "the Rest of Canada" (ROC).

Stabilization Aspects of a Common Currency

Independence of the EuroFed

Price stability, according to the European Community (EC), is the "*sine qua non* for economic and monetary union."[1] Therefore, the Europeans are proposing rather drastic measures to ensure that the

---

1 Commission of the European Communities, *Economic and Monetary Union* (Brussels, 1990), p. 12.

anticipated EuroFed will be unconstrained in its pursuit of price stability. Toward this end, the first measure that the Europeans are contemplating is a complete severing of the link between the existing national central banks and their respective governments. Once this occurs, the EC will create a new institution — the EuroFed — that would have a "federal structure". Specifically, the EuroFed would be placed under the "authority of a Council composed of the 12 governors of the Community central banks and of a smaller number of members from the EuroFed itself."[2] Once again, the emphasis is on independence:

> In performing their duties, the European Central Bank, a central bank of a Member State and members of their decision-making bodies shall neither seek nor take instructions from the institutions of the Community or its Member States or from any other body.
> The Community and the Member States shall not seek to influence the European Central Bank, the central banks of the Member States and the members of their decision-making bodies in the performance of their tasks and shall respect their independence. To that end, the Member States shall amend, where necessary, legislation governing relations between their central banks and their national governments.[3]

To be sure, these concepts are not yet cast in stone. Indeed, the recent resignation of Bundesbank President Karl Otto Poehl and the policy issues surrounding the selection of his successor have raised the issue of whether the independence issue of a Eurofed will (*à la* Poehl) continue to dominate or whether the more political approach of the Bank of France will become ascendent. For the purposes of this study, I shall assume the former.

Another aspect of this independence relates to the prohibition of bailouts: "The European Central Bank may under no circum-

---

2 Ibid.

3 Commission of the European Communities, "Draft Treaty Amending the Treaty Establishing the European Economic Community with a View to Achieving Economic and Monetary Union" (Brussels, December 10, 1990), Article 106a, p.10.

stances grant to the Community or to any one of its Member States or to any public body a loan or any other credit facility intended to make good a budget deficit."[4] However, the constraints go much beyond severing the EuroFed-member state relationship. In the case of imbalances, a member state would not even be allowed to benefit from an unconditional guarantee with respect to its public debt either from the Community or from another member state.[5]

Deficit Constraints

In principle, the EC's member states will remain fiscally autonomous. In practice, however, this "freedom" will be subjected to the Community goal of price stability. Apart from measures already alluded to, the principal way that this will occur is through deficit control:

> Excessive [member state] budget deficits may endanger the stability-oriented monetary policy. As a matter of principle, excessive budget deficits therefore must be avoided and this should be stated in the Treaty [it *is* stated in the Draft Treaty —T.J.C.]. In practice, the judgment whether a deficit is excessive is related to the sustainability of the fiscal position, which cannot be evaluated in isolation from an overall assessment of the economic situation and development, and should therefore be an integral part of multilateral surveillance. Nevertheless, some yardstick would seem necessary for the identification of excessive deficits. Despite its definitional shortcomings, the golden rule of public finance, i.e., that public borrowing shall not exceed investment expenditure, appears the most satisfactory from an analytical point of view and is the only one widely applied in existing federations. Complementary to this rule, other objective criteria, such as deficit and debt to GNP ratios might prove helpful in this context. These rules and criteria will have to be laid down in the Council regulation covering multilateral surveillance.[6]

---

4 Ibid.

5 Commission of the European Communities, *Economic and Monetary Union*, p. 26.

6 Ibid., p. 25.

This is not mere rhetoric. All member nations would be borrowing in the new European currency, not their own currency. The fear is that the removal of "currency risk" from any one country's debt obligations might encourage even more borrowing on the part of several of them. And in 1989, five of the 12 member states had fiscal deficits of more than 5 percent of GNP, with Greece (17.6 percent) and Italy (10.2 percent) leading the way. Thus, national fiscal flexibility, at least in terms of deficit freedom, will be constrained to ensure that these actions do not compromise the actions of the EuroFed in terms of pursuing price stability.

Fiscal autonomy would be curtailed in a second way: member states would be constrained from, or at least closely monitored when, borrowing abroad in a currency other than the ECU.

How this relates to a CQEMU will be addressed later. I turn first to the adjustment impacts of a common currency.

Adjustment Aspects of a Common Currency

The EC concern here relates to the sustainability of a single European currency. In particular, what arrangements are necessary to ensure that, in the face of *country-specific* (not Community-wide) economic shocks, member states will stick with the common currency arrangements and dictates?

It is not difficult to see why and how "opting out" of the common currency could become appealing. Consider the following scenario. Country X is hit by an internal or external shock that leaves it reeling. By definition, exchange-rate solutions are ruled out. So are any and all explicit protectionist policies, as well as those that are even implicitly protectionist — that is, those that would subsidize or favor "home" industry. While fiscal stabilization remains, the likelihood is, however, that country X would already be in fiscal trouble and could well be running into the "deficit guidelines" imposed by the price-stability goal. Moreover, loan or borrowing guarantees by the Community or any other member state are also precluded.

Essentially, all that remain are labor market strategies — wage flexibility and/or labor mobility. Even here, however, there are constraints. Incomes policies are not particularly effective when the problem is structural. But, at least there is some room to maneuver here. In terms of labor mobility, while the EC endorses migration in search of employment, it is much less excited about substantial migration triggered by unemployment at home and by the appeal of social security policies in richer member states. It is almost as if there is an implicit goal that, other things equal, the Portuguese ought to remain in Portugal. (As a relevant aside, if this is an EC goal, Canada can clearly show them how to do this!)

This potential for unemployment-push, welfare-pull mobility strikes at the core of the EC concern. Specifically, there are few of the "federal-type" adjustment policies in the EC — such as cross-Community income taxation and programs such as equalization payments — that characterize Canada's federation. The question addressed by the EC is whether or not the EEMU is sustainable in the absence of these forms of cross-Community macro redistribution.

In response to these concerns, the EC has already conceded that some version of a Community "adjustment fund" is appropriate, probably modeled after the approach of the International Monetary Fund (IMF) — namely, that any funds offered to member states would require a series of adjustment policies on the part of the recipient:

> A special financial support scheme would be provided for....The scheme would be activated when major economic problems arise in one or several Member States or when economic convergence calls for a particular Community effort alongside national adjustment strategies in the sense of positive conditionality. The initiative for activating the scheme could come from the Member State concerned as well as from the Commission. The Council would decide the conditions and details of the support when a case arises, including the need for coherence with multilateral surveillance concerning budget deficits. The support could be given through grants from the Community budget or through loans from a Community financial instrument.[7]

---

7 Ibid.

In turn, this would imply access by the Community to some tax base or bases and to some borrowing authority — although in terms of the former, some Community monies might be generated by the "seigniorage" associated with the operations of the EuroFed.[8]

Canada, of course, has many such instruments currently in place, ranging from direct instruments such as equalization payments, regional development grants, and subsidies to overcome economic hardships (such as the plight of grain farmers), to more indirect instruments such as the operations of the income tax systems and unemployment insurance (UI). Presumably, all of these would disappear between Quebec and ROC under independence and then economic and monetary union, or at least they would be subject to confederal decisionmaking. Is this likely to imply that the sustainability of the common currency would be jeopardized? Can there be a sustainable CQEMU without some common UI programs or some inter-"country" redistribution systems? Moreover, if adjustment funds (with conditions) become a part of a CQEMU, how would these be financed — on a 50/50 Quebec-ROC basis or in terms of population or GNP shares? Addressing the Canadian reality in terms of a monetary union is the purpose of the next section.

A Canada-Quebec Monetary Union

A "CanaFed"?

In his brief to the Bélanger-Campeau Commission, economist Rodrigue Tremblay argues that the preferred option is a "CanaFed", modeled after the proposed EuroFed. Quebec would establish a

---

8 Seigniorage is the term applied to the returns that are inherent in the monopoly to issue currency. For example, Canadians and chartered banks hold about $25 billion in currency — either in terms of bills or, for the banks, in deposits with the Bank of Canada. No interest is paid on these liabilities. As a result, the Bank has a corresponding portfolio of $25 billion, mostly in government bills and bonds. The Bank's profits ($2.4 billion in the most recent year) are turned over to the federal government. This is seigniorage.

Bank of Quebec that would be its equivalent of the Bank of Canada. The governors and deputy governors of these two banks would then form the management committee of the CanaFed. As an alternative, he suggests that Quebec's minister of finance, rather than a formal Bank of Quebec, could nominate representatives to the CanaFed.[9]

Taking some liberties with Tremblay's proposal, why not have the finance ministries of both Quebec and Canada name an equivalent number of directors — with the ministers of finance as nonvoting members — to the present Bank of Canada, which, in turn, would become the CanaFed? This "constitutionalization" of a formal monetary union is, according to Tremblay, one of the necessary conditions that must be in place before Quebec would accept its appropriate share of the Canadian debt — which he assumes to be in the order of 25 percent.

A second condition would be to transfer all powers of taxation to Quebec. This again is in line with the European model in the sense that there would be no parliament associated with the superstructure. (True, Europe has a parliament, but it has few powers at present.) Presumably, the seigniorage would more than cover the administration of the CanaFed, with the excess devoted to covering some of the costs of the economic union or to debt reduction. Tremblay views such a formal arrangement as absolutely essential until the "Canadian" debt is retired. Indeed, there is no reason why this arrangement could not continue in perpetuity.

Tremblay's second and less preferred option is an "informal agreement" that would allow the transfer of taxing powers and debt from Canada to Quebec. Over a transition period — say, two years — Canada would gradually transfer taxing powers and the debt share to Quebec. During this period, Quebec would establish its own central bank with the responsibility for issuing a Quebec currency. The value of that new currency, however, would be fixed at par with

---

9 Rodrigue Tremblay, "Le statut politique et constitutionnel du Québec," in Quebec, Commission on the Political and Constitutional Future of Quebec [Bélanger-Campeau Commission], *Les avis des spécialistes invités à répondre aux huit questions posées par la Commission* [Background papers], vol.4 (Quebec, 1991).

the Canadian dollar; this parity would then be defended *jointly* by ROC and Quebec.

Neither of these proposals would sit well with ROC, the first because Quebec would have a full and equal share in the management of the CanaFed and the second because overall monetary policy would have to be devoted to maintain Quebec-ROC currency parity, probably at the expense of price stability. This latter is a version of the German unification problem. Former Bundesbank President Karl Otto Poehl has admitted publicly that German monetary unification was a disaster because it took place at much too high an exchange rate for the former East German currency. This was, however, a political decision, in which the traditionally fiercely independent Bundesbank was simply swept along.

Past history may not be relevant, but it is at least of interest to note, as Tremblay does, that under the 1841 *Act of Union*, the debt of Upper Canada (Ontario) was taken over in its entirety by the two provinces even though Lower Canada (Quebec) had no debt.[10] Moreover, while Quebec had 1½ times the population of Ontario, an equal number of members from Upper and Lower Canada sat in the new parliament.

What is inescapable, however, and what ROC has to come to terms with, is that if Quebec agrees to take its appropriate share of the debt, *and if this debt is denominated in Canadian dollars*, then Quebec ought to have some say in how the Canadian dollar is managed or, as noted earlier, be given some guarantee as to the limits of this liability. Even though Quebecers now hold about 18 percent of the outstanding federal debt — which, intriguingly, is close to the 18.5 percent share of the federal debt that the Bélanger-Campeau background paper recommends as appropriate for Quebec to assume — it really would not be possible to assign this portion of the debt directly to Quebec to be denominated in a new Quebec currency. Holders of Canada Savings Bonds (CSBs) in Quebec are not different than holders of CSBs elsewhere in the country: they presumably

10 Ibid., p. 1050.

would cash in their bonds immediately if they foresaw a potential capital loss. More on this later. Indeed, more also on what is emerging as an alternative to a formal monetary union — namely, that Quebec would simply continue to "use" the Canadian dollar.

Adjustment Problems of a Monetary Union

Appropriately, the Allaire Report recognizes that there is a need for fiscal coordination in a monetary union:

> Clearly, the monetary union will be viable only if the regions' budgetary policies are consistent. Uncoordinated and diverging policies would only work to compromise monetary stability and hence the conduct of a common monetary policy. The need for coordination is particularly important since the budget of the common authorities will be strictly limited, accounting for only a low proportion of total public spending, and will be constrained by rules such as a limitation on borrowing authority.[11]

But is there any evidence that Quebec would ever subject its overall fiscal framework to the dictates of a CanaFed? This would again be an example of independence leading to Pyrrhic powers.

As an important aside, the EC's focus only on the fiscal stances of deficit nations appears to me to be far too narrow. As I have argued elsewhere,[12] Canada's battle against wage and price inflation would have been facilitated greatly if, over the 1983–88 period, booming Ontario had "saved" rather than "spent" at least some of its fiscal dividend. That is, even though Ontario's deficit over this period would not qualify as high (in terms of the EC's guidelines) it was nonetheless too high in terms of the ongoing macro policy. In the event, Ontario "superheated" its own economy and forced the Bank of Canada's hand in terms of ratcheting up interest rates. However,

---

11 Quebec Liberal Party, Constitutional Committee, *A Quebec Free to Choose* (Quebec, January 28, 1991), p. 42.

12 Thomas J. Courchene, "Zero Means Almost Nothing: Towards a Preferable Inflation and Macroeconomic Policy," *Queen's Quarterly* 97 (1990): 543–561.

the recent Ontario deficit is exactly what the EC guidelines are designed to deter!

This aside, what happens in a CQEMU if Quebec is hit by a province-specific economic shock? This could arise for all sorts of reasons — for example, a temporary collapse in business confidence arising because shareholders of major Canadian companies — such as Bell, Canadian Pacific, Air Canada, Via Rail, and some chartered banks — decide to pull their headquarters out of Quebec. indeed, they would be required to do so in order to remain Canadian companies. More generally, and more likely, suppose that, on the patriation of taxing powers and its share of the debt, Quebec finds that the common currency is "overvalued" with respect to its economic position *vis-à-vis* ROC and the United States. What can it do under a CQEMU? The answer is almost nothing — no subsidies, no protectionist barriers, no changes in tariffs. Two policy options do remain: an internal wage devaluation to render itself more competitive or a revving up of government deficits to increase aggregate demand. There is, of course, a third option: Quebecers could simply emigrate.

How does a central bank — a CanaFed — respond to this? One could envision a European-type adjustment fund whereby the CQEMU would transfer adjustment funds to Quebec under IMF-type requirements and directives relating to how these funds are to be deployed. This would probably not sit well with either Quebec or ROC. A second type of response might be that the directors of the CanaFed appointed by Quebec would push for monetary ease — presumably in the form of lower interest rates and a lower dollar. Again, ROC would resist. Third, Quebec could opt out of the CQEMU and establish its own currency, with potentially dramatic costs to both Quebec and ROC.

The basic problem in all of this is that the European experience is not particularly useful as a guide. The EC member states have had "relatively fixed" exchange rates for a long period now, so that the appropriate exchange rates for moving to a common currency are more or less market determined. (Even so, the monetary implications of German unification presumably will call into question the desirability of, or at least delay, the implementation of a EuroFed and a single European currency.) More to the point, there is no European equivalent of the $400 billion Canadian debt overhang. Even if international capital markets maintained their confidence in "Canada" over this period, it is impossible to assess *a priori* whether parity between ROC and Quebec — that is, a single currency — would make any economic sense. And if capital markets become jittery, parity could well become unmanageable.

Chapter 5

Assessing a CQEMU

Feasibility

Administrative

Administratively, a Canada-Quebec economic and monetary union (CQEMU) is certainly feasible. Probably the best way to proceed would be to assume that the House of Commons would become the parliament for "the Rest of Canada" (ROC), with the Assemblée nationale playing the same role for Quebec.[1] (What happens to the Senate presumably would be up to ROC, since Quebec would not be part of it.) Each parliament would be fully sovereign, except for the dictates of the CQEMU.

This administrative superstructure, both for the economic union and the new joint central bank (the CanaFed) would be confederal — representatives, not elected members, from ROC and Quebec would constitute the management of the CQEMU bureaucracy. Funding would come in part from CanaFed seigniorage. Beyond this, the superstructure would need funds to service and pay down the debt — presumably, this would come from taxes imposed on ROC and Quebec in accordance with the debt-sharing arrangements. If some "adjustment funds" were put in place, these too would have to come from levies on ROC and Quebec. How to "allocate" these levies across Quebec and ROC brings us into the realm of "political" feasibility, to which I now turn.

---

1 This is the approach suggested by Léon Dion, "Léon Dion propose un régime confédéral," *La Presse* (Montreal), January 11, 1991, p. B-3.

Political

Would ROC ever agree to a bipolar CQEMU, where it and Quebec had equal powers? Obviously, in this case, Quebec would be required to share equally in the costs as well, except for the debt and deficit arrangements. Would Quebec agree to this? I do not know the answers to these questions, but my guess is that they would be no.

My colleague Dan Soberman argues that bipolar arrangements between unequal partners are inherently unstable:

> Bipolar monetary unions with each party having an equal say, that is, each having a veto, are rare — if indeed there are any at all — because they are inherently unstable. The risks of impasse and frustration leading to paralysis mean they are unlikely to last. Moreover, the inducements to enter into such an arrangement in the first place must be negligible: the larger and wealthier member state would ordinarily have little incentive to give the smaller partner a veto, thus limiting its own autonomy for no net gain; conversely, for the smaller partner there would be little incentive to agree to be a supplicant that ultimately had no role other than to adhere to the decisions of the dominant member. The scenario is rather stark — either a veto and the unpalatable risks of impasse, or one party being a mere supplicant with the danger of regularly being the loser in any disagreement....
>
> Indeed, in any expanded two-party arrangement between Quebec and the rest-of-Canada — a common market that comprised a free trade area, customs union, integrated transportation policy and free movement of the factors of production — granting to an independent Quebec full equality in the form of a veto in all these areas would be even more unlikely; the higher the level of economic integration that the parties contemplate, the more unpalatable such a bipolar arrangement becomes.[2]

The major point here is that a bipolar relationship with unequal partners will lead to fears of domination on the part of the weaker party and the fear of encumbrances on the part of the dominant party.

---

2 Daniel Soberman, "European Integration: Are There Lessons for Canada?" in Ronald L. Watts and Douglas M. Brown, eds., *Options for a New Canada* (Toronto: University of Toronto Press, 1991), pp. 202–203.

One potential counter to this is the Canada-U.S. Free Trade Agreement (FTA), which is far more unequal in terms of the partners than any CQEMU. If the FTA is feasible, and presumably stable, why not a CQEMU? The answer, at least from my perspective, is that the FTA and the CQEMU are quite different animals. Where they are similar — namely, in monitoring and adjudicating the various treaty or administrative provisions — a CQEMU might be politically viable and stable. A CQEMU, however, is much more than a FTA, in the sense that, unlike the latter, it would involve critical *policy* decisions that would have to be addressed by the economic and monetary union superstructure. Apart from the initial negotiations that would necessarily involve subsidy pacts and government (and hydro) purchasing, these policy decisions would include issues relating to appropriate deficits, appropriate monetary policy, a schedule for paying down the joint debt, incorporating emerging environmental values into the CQEMU, and a host of other delicate and difficult issues. Here, I think, Soberman is probably correct.

One additional point needs to be made here. The most critical determinant of feasibility on both the political and economic sides is the *process* by which Quebec and ROC approach a CQEMU. If a CQEMU arises because earnest and lengthy negotiations relating to a renewed federalism fail to achieve the needed degree of mutual accommodation and, as a result, Quebec and ROC agree to negotiate the friendliest of partings, then a CQEMU may be feasible. If, however, Quebec declares its sovereignty through a unilateral declaration of independence or, equivalently, by voting down an offer that ROC deems to be accommodating, then there is probably little hope of negotiating the complex and, in many areas, interventionist superstructure needed for a CQEMU.

Economic

Even under the best of processes, the economic viability of a meaningful CQEMU would be highly questionable. It is not necessary to reproduce the many problematic issues on this front that have been raised earlier. Nonetheless, it is instructive to reiterate that the issues would revolve around the rights of "successor" and "predecessor" states, the sharing of the debt, the appropriateness of a one-to-one exchange rate between Quebec and ROC, the utter inflexibility (except for monetary expansion) in terms of adjustment options for either Quebec or ROC in the face of impact or subsequent economic shocks, as well as the likelihood that a full-blown CQEMU would emasculate Quebec society of its innate advantage — which is, to put it briefly, that Quebec is a North American economy with a distinctive non-North American approach to political economy.

Thus, the tentative conclusion that I draw from all this is that a full-blown CQEMU is unlikely to be feasible politically or economically. This answer, however, is not fully satisfactory because, if Quebec does secede, *some* arrangement between Quebec and ROC obviously would come into being and, by definition, therefore, would be feasible. What these arrangements might be are addressed in Chapter 6.

Desirability

Suppose, however, that a CQEMU can be negotiated. Is this likely to be desirable? Before I attempt to suggest some answers, it is important to note that the comparison here is between a CQEMU on the one hand and two sovereign states with, say, FTAs on the other. Renewed federalism is not an option for purposes of the present discussion. Moreover, the assumption is that the difficult issues — such as debt sharing and the administration of the economic and monetary union — have been resolved satisfactorily.

At the level of economics and, in particular, in terms of reducing the economic uncertainty associated with the breakup, the answer is surely "yes, a CQEMU *is* desirable". International capital markets presumably would be pacified, especially if the CQEMU were to embody the Allaire Report's thrust to highlight debt reduction. The disruption of east-west trade flows would be reduced to the inescapable (and politically triggered) minimum. Moreover, a successful

CQEMU presumably would forestall or at least delay initiatives such as shifts of corporate headquarters. In other words, the scenario is one of a friendly divorce where both parties take immediate and, indeed, magnanimous steps to attempt to ensure each other's economic viability.

Phrased in this way, desirability is really not at issue. The problem is that, except under the most exceptional of circumstances, one cannot get there from here.

In political or political economy terms, however, it is not obvious that a CQEMU is desirable. My hunch is that a full-blown CQEMU would mean more, not less, "entanglement" between ROC and Quebec. Language and cultural issues might assume a lower profile — although even this is not certain — but the administrative and legal process likely would bite across a wide range of policy areas for which there will be no recourse except arbitration by supranational and confederal dispute-settlement mechanisms. Surely, this is not what the emerging "let them go" or "bon voyage" mentality in ROC has in mind.

What Would Be In It for Quebec?

On the surface, it would appear that a CQEMU is even less likely to satisfy the aspirations of Québécois. However, I can think of two scenarios in which a CQEMU would be appealing to Quebec.

Scenario 1

The first is that Quebec's overriding goal is to become "sovereign" in the symbolic sense. Once it achieves this goal, it would then be quite willing to turn control over aspects of much of its economic policy to a CQEMU, because that is the way in which globalization is driving the system in any event.

I do not want to downplay this scenario. What it means is that Quebec would enjoy all the prestigious trappings of the world's newest nation state — emissaries abroad, foreign embassies in Quebec City or Montreal or Hull, and membership in the United Nations, possibly NATO, and countless other international organizations. Moreover, some of this symbolism is probably "negative" — that is, directed against ROC. In their view, Quebecers said "yes" to Canada and renewed federalism in 1980 only to find their province excluded from the *Constitution Act, 1982.* Quebec again opted for Canada in the 1987 Meech Lake Accord and repeated its commitment in 1990 in Meech II. But ROC again said "No" to Quebec, replete with the high-profile, much-replayed Quebec-flag-stomping affair in Brockville. It may well be true that, for ROC, the turning point in the Meech Lake exercise was Premier Bourassa's resort to the notwithstanding clause in connection with Bill 178, the language-of-signs legislation. Nonetheless, ROC ignores at its peril that some of what Quebec is now about is "getting back" at Canada. In this context, a separate Quebec would almost automatically imply that ROC would lose its status as a member of the Group-of-Seven major industrial countries — although a CQEMU might keep it in. Moreover, the sometimes-proffered notion that a sovereign Quebec would no longer wield influence in *la francophonie* is patently foolish. What Ottawa ought to be saying is that Canada's (or ROC's) role in *la francophonie* would become nonexistent! I find it hard to imagine that Quebec's role or influence *per se* would decline.

In any event, the remainder of the scenario would be that, for Quebec, with "sovereignty in the bag", so to speak, and with control in principle over all taxation and spending laws, not much is sacrificed by a full-blown economic union, since this curtailing of powers is inevitable in terms of how the international economy is evolving. In any event, the United States will force much of this on Quebec in the context of the FTA.

There is, of course, the possibility that discussion in Quebec of a CQEMU is largely a marketing ploy by the Parti Québécois in order to enhance popular support for sovereignty — that is, to minimize the economic uncertainty that would attend a breakup. Nevertheless, I believe that Quebecers will *not* be satisfied with a CQEMU that would ride herd on much of the dynamism that made their economy flourish in the 1980s. Even a cursory glance at the many background briefs (by "expert witnesses") prepared for the Bélanger-Campeau Commission reveals a sense of confidence and optimism in Quebec and Quebecers. Implicit in these briefs is that an independent and unencumbered Quebec can put these societal accomplishments and attributes to work on a much broader scale. Among these *atouts* are:

- a rich resource base;
- an ideal locational entrée to the United States;
- a high degree of Quebec ownership of the corporate sector;
- an efficient financial-institution network;
- an industrial strategy characterized by a close working arrangement among business, finance, government, and, on occasion, even labor; and
- a degree of societal cohesion unmatched in North America, which many Quebecers believe will serve them well in the fast-changing global environment.

More generally, what will increasingly matter in the global economy is how effective economic "systems" are, where systems are the combination of such things as institutions, entrepreneurship, attitudes, cooperation between industry and government, and human capital formation.[4] Quebec will, in my view, not want its "system" constrained by a CQEMU nor will it want to be constrained from developing special links with *la francophonie*, with the United States — particularly the northeastern states — and with Europe.

Scenario 2

This leads to the second scenario within which Quebec might find a CQEMU to be desirable — namely, that a CQEMU would really be an essential temporary economic safety net in the difficult and

---

4 Daniel Latouche, "La stratégie québécoise dans le nouvel ordre économique et politique international," in Quebec, Commission on the Political and Constitutional Future of Quebec [Bélanger-Campeau Commission], *Les avis des spécialistes invités à répondre aux huit questions posées par la Commission* [Background papers], vol.4 (Quebec, 1991), p. 616

uncertain transition from a Canadian province to a fully independent country. Once the joint debt is paid down to a digestible level and once the world community has recognized the viability of an independent Quebec, the obvious next move would be outright sovereignty. If outright independence is Quebec's goal, it seems to me hard to make a case, from Quebec's vantage point, against a CQEMU as a desirable but temporary halfway house.

Initial reaction on ROC's part to this general approach would clearly be negative. But how would ROC know that this is intended to be temporary? Intriguingly, however, in a sense this halfway house would probably serve ROC's interests more than Quebec's, since it is ROC that is completely unprepared politically, psychologically, and even economically for a quick exit by Quebec.[5]

Given that a CQEMU probably would not be on, what are the likely implications for Quebec and the rest of Canada if Quebec nonetheless does opt for independence?

---

5 I pursue this line of reasoning in the concluding chapter.

Chapter 6

Quebec Independence without a CQEMU

There is no question but that a declaration of independence by Quebec without the prospects of a Canada-Quebec economic and monetary union (CQEMU) would deliver a substantial and immediate economic shock to Quebec — and to "the Rest of Canada" (ROC).

A negotiated transition period would appear to be absolutely essential, during which disentanglement would take place — for example, the phasing out of equalization payments and the phasing in of tax powers and debt sharing. During this phase-in period, Quebec would have to negotiate free trade agreements (FTAs) with both Canada and the United States. Despite the problems that might be associated with these negotiations, FTAs in some version *would*, in my view, emerge.

Likewise, Quebec would use this period to develop its own external commercial policy and in the process to decide whether, as a society, to bear the costs of maintaining protection for textile workers and dairy farmers, for example. The transition presumably would also involve substantial movements of people both ways — Quebecers working in Ottawa might wish to come to the new Quebec, although they presumably would have the right to maintain their positions provided they resided in, or moved to, ROC. Offsetting this would be a renewed exodus of English-speaking Quebecers and, as already noted, the likelihood of the migration of major corporate headquarters from Montreal.

It is not obvious what one can or should say about these transition costs, given the degree of uncertainty that attends them. A difficult scenario — but not the worst-case scenario — would be one where the United States hangs tough on an FTA and where the transition problems undermine the confidence of the Quebec business elite. Obviously, all of this would be compounded by a "bitter" breakup. A much more pleasant scenario would involve the negotiation of favorable FTAs with the United States and ROC. Intriguingly, if the Americans perceive that the breakup could become dysfunctional economically, they might — at least initially — act in ways that would tend to maintain the status quo in terms of trading arrangements and to pacify international capital markets. Thus, while the transition for Quebec would doubtlessly be difficult, just how difficult is beyond my, and I think most observers', ability to ascertain.

It is important to recognize that the Bélanger-Campeau Commission's Secretariat, in its own background papers, appears to be moving away from the concept of a CQEMU — particularly the monetary union components. The assumption now appears to be that Quebec would simply continue to *use* the Canadian dollar. This would not preclude a formal monetary union, but it would assure Quebecers of the continuation of this key part of their "Canadian" experience. More to the point, this assumption is an "official" recognition that concerns of stability or viability would dominate the transition and that "anchors" such as the Canadian dollar would be important, domestically and internationally. Special arrangements would have to be devised in order that cheque clearings and payments flows could continue roughly as they do now.

ROC presumably would not agree with the Bélanger-Campeau Secretariat's proposition that Quebec be compensated for using the Canadian dollar — because it would enhance ROC's seigniorage. But beyond this, Quebec's use of the Canadian dollar seems to be feasible, and the major roadblock here would be complete recalcitrance on the part of ROC. Should ROC somehow prevent Quebec's access to the Canadian dollar — perhaps through precluding correspondent relationships with the Canadian chartered banks — then the United States might offer its currency to Quebec. Were this to occur, I believe that ROC would quickly have to link itself to the U.S. dollar as well.

This aside, the point here is that maintaining the Canadian dollar would surely serve to enhance Quebec's economic prospects during the transition period, although from precisely which depressed level is unclear, as noted earlier. It would also facilitate the maintenance of existing trade flows, since there would be no "currency transactions" costs. Finally, this approach might serve to pacify international financial markets, since, as long as the Bank of Canada was committed to price stability, so Quebec would be as well, given that it would have no say in Bank of Canada monetary management. Phrased somewhat differently, in the transition there would be no (or much less) tendency for Quebec to inflate its way out of any problem because it would have no ability to do so. This, however, is also one of the costs of such a scenario — not so much that it could not resort to inflation but rather that it would be locking itself into an economic framework that, like the former East Germany's, might be entirely inappropriate.

In any event, the possibility of "using" the Canadian or U.S. dollars would represent an important degree of freedom for an independent Quebec, because it would allow the new nation a version of a monetary union *without* the necessity of a full-blown economic union.

However, several important questions arise. First, is this currency "arrangement" likely to be stable? Second, is it likely that ROC would find it advantageous? Third, would this effectively erode Quebec's "sovereignty"? In order to address these and other issues, it is instructive to begin by noting that the Canadian dollar would, in effect, become a "reserve" currency. The U.S. dollar is the world's premier reserve currency. Some countries (Panama, Liberia) even "use" the U.S. dollar in the very way that Quebec might use the Canadian dollar. In my view, however, the Panamanian and Liberian examples are not particularly instructive, since these countries are too small to have any effect on the conduct of U.S. monetary policy.

The Quebec-Canada arrangement would be quite different. It would imply that roughly one-quarter of the Canadian dollar area would be outside the sphere of influence of the Canadian macro authorities. What would happen if Quebec began to run significant balance-of-payments deficits? (Or surpluses, for that matter, although I will focus on the former.) Canadian dollars would flow out of Quebec and into the hands of "foreigners". If the balance-of-payments deficit was with ROC, the dollar inflow would increase the money supply in ROC and presumably would trigger tightening by the Bank of Canada. Alternatively, Quebec institutions could float debt in ROC to "replenish" their money supply. The "appropriate" — along gold-standard-adjustment lines — response would be an internal one: Quebec wages and domestic prices should decline in order to correct the balance-of-payments deficit. The Bank of Canada, however, would have no leverage over Quebec in terms of that "appropriate" response. (Admittedly, it now has little leverage over Ontario's budget stance!)

If, on the other hand, the balance-of-payments deficit was with the United States, U.S. exporters would go to the Canadian foreign-exchange "window" and convert these Canadian dollars into U.S. dollars. Under this scenario, Quebec's balance-of-payments deficits would erode Canada's foreign-exchange reserves. Again, the Bank of Canada would have to tighten monetary policy — which would also apply to Quebec — even though monetary tightening might be inappropriate for ROC. Even worse, suppose that Quebec's external balance was such that international capital markets came to believe that the only way out was for Quebec to adopt its own currency and engineer a devaluation. What would this do to the value of the Canadian dollar on international markets?

While these are appropriate questions, I do not know what the appropriate answers are. What is clearly *inappropriate* is the assertion by the Bélanger-Campeau Commission that if Quebec decided to "use" the Canadian dollar, the province would merit compensation for the extra seigniorage that would accrue to ROC. My hunch, and it is only a hunch, is that this relationship would not be stable. ROC would demand some control over Quebec's policies if they compromised the Bank of Canada's desired monetary policy. Alternatively, ROC and the Bank could make the currency-sharing arrangement problematical through a variety of technical and regulatory initiatives. While Quebec might feel that having no say over monetary policy would not be much different than the status quo, my guess is that a separate Quebec currency would be virtually inevitable.

If Quebec were to opt for its own currency, this would obviously introduce a new element of instability into what likely would already be an unstable environment. Any instability, however, would also carry over to ROC, since one-quarter of its currency area would disappear.

But consider the following scenario. Suppose Quebec realizes that there will be costs associated with separation and decides it is willing to bear them. One way in which it might be willing to do so is through a currency depreciation in the context of introducing its new currency, the Quebec *dollard* — after Dollard Des Ormeaux or, if one wishes, because it will be a *dollar d*evalued. This devaluation would, however, be internal. By this I mean that on, say, the *Fête de Dollard*, Quebec might announce that henceforth all wages will fall by 10 percent — and foreign prices will go up by 10 percent — and will then be denominated in dollards. Then Quebec will issue dollards at parity with Canadian dollars. Initially, the new Bank of Quebec would simply act like a currency board, not a bank — all dollards would be backed fully by Canadian dollars or Canadian-dollar-denominated liabilities for a transition period sufficiently long for the dollard to be accepted domestically and internationally.

This initiative would accomplish three goals. First, by locking on, on a one-to-one basis, to the Canadian dollar, it would also lock on to the Bank of Canada's price-stability credibility. This assumes, of course, that the dollard would not be further devalued, which, in turn, is why the transition period of a currency board or currency exchange — prior to a full-fledged Bank of Quebec — would probably be needed. Second, by having an *internal* devaluation, Quebec would still ensure a one-for-one exchange rate for dollards and dollars that would reduce transactions costs. Third, and very significantly, Quebec would have a competitive edge in terms of market access to both ROC and the United States. And there would be nothing that ROC could do about this! It could not devalue with regard to the dollard because of Quebec's fixing its currency on a one-to-one basis, backed fully by Canadian dollars.

There is another variant of this, which might be even more preferable for Quebec — although more problematical for ROC. Specifically, as was evident from Table 1 in Chapter 2, the optimal currency areas for Canada's regions increasingly are north-south, not east-west. This being the case, Quebec might, after its internal devaluation, want to latch on to the U.S. dollar rather than to the Canadian dollar on a one-to-one basis. The result would be the same — Quebec would have engineered an effective 10 percent devaluation against ROC and the United States. In this case, the Bank of Canada and the government of ROC would be free to follow Quebec's lead and devalue relative to the United States as well.

The critical issue here is whether the truncated currency area for the Canadian dollar would be viable enough to allow for continued exchange-rate flexibility or whether ROC would also have to link itself more formally to the U.S. dollar. As an aside, I would find this a plus, since I have argued that Canada should have fixed the dollar at 80 cents U.S. when the FTA came into being.[1]

No doubt, some readers will view the above scenario as overly optimistic in terms of Quebec's prospects. It should be remembered, however, that this is meant primarily as an examination of some of Quebec's options on the currency front, not a suggestion that the overall transition will in any way be either easy or short.

Nonetheless, if one assumes that Quebec could make it through the transition, it then does become possible to paint a more rosy picture. At this point, Quebec and Quebecers could begin to put their societal attributes to work with considerable benefit. They would be subject to "national treatment", not to the centralizing aspects of a CQEMU, which, as I have already noted, would deprive Quebec of many of the benefits of sovereignty. Quebec would obviously make

---

1 Thomas J. Courchene, "Zero Means Almost Nothing: Towards a Preferable Inflation and Macroeconomic Policy," *Queen's Quarterly* 97 (1990): 543–561.

overtures to Ontario for closer economic integration along the Quebec City-Windsor corridor. These would be more in the nature of "business pacts" and might be easier to negotiate than formal economic union arrangements. Finally, and this might be strategically important, Quebec would attempt to capitalize on the fact that it is really more like a continental European economy with a beachhead in North America.

Recapitulation

What I draw from all of this is that, for Quebec, sovereignty with a CQEMU probably would not be feasible over the short term and, in any event, probably would not be desirable, since Quebec would find it too constraining over the longer term. Independence with separate FTAs with ROC and the United States as a fallback option might have some enviable longer-term consequences, but it is not clear that Quebec could ever make it through the transition; alternatively, the transition might be very long. However, using the Canadian (or U.S.) dollar to generate an unofficial monetary union could be helpful here. So might the introduction of a Quebec dollar if it were done along the lines advocated above or, more generally, if it were introduced in a manner such that it took cognizance of aspects having to do with price stability and transactions costs.

Nonetheless, to anticipate the analysis in the remainder of the study, my overall conclusion is that Quebec could be much better off with a renewed federalism — although by the very manner in which the analysis has been structured, this conclusion tends to emerge as the least problematical or least risky option. In Chapter 8, however, I argue that renewed federalism is Quebec's first-best option.

This, then, shifts the focus back to ROC. How much of the emerging "bon voyage" sentiment in ROC is triggered by a belief that, in the final analysis, Quebec will stay because independence is too great a gamble? How much reflects a view that Quebec's exit would not saddle ROC with substantial costs? And how much represents a coalescing of a new ROC identity and the accompanying will to develop a society in its own likeness? These are now emerging as the critical issues in Canada's constitutional crisis, since Quebec has already revealed its hand. Addressing these questions in any meaningful way is well beyond the scope of this study. Nonetheless, the purpose of the next chapter is to address some of the costs that Quebec's separation would or could impose on ROC. This focus is appropriate, since, as noted earlier, most of the discussion of the costs of a breakup has thus far centered on Quebec.

Chapter 7

Quebec Independence and "the Rest of Canada"

The Quebec-Will-Not-Go Scenario

Apart from the arguments made in the previous chapter that an exit by Quebec would be highly problematical, proponents of the Quebec-will-not-go view buttress their argument in several ways.

Two of these are political/constitutional. The first is that, constitutionally, Quebec *cannot* go: there is no provision in the Constitution for secession. I do not have the expertise to comment on this. The second is, in my view, more problematical: if the Grand Council of the Cree were to opt for Canada in a referendum held in the same time frame as Quebecers voted for sovereignty, it is not obvious that Quebec could exit with its existing boundaries intact, since Ungava was given to Quebec, as a province, in 1912. Again I defer to the experts.

In a sense, it is inappropriate to raise such political quandaries in the context of what is, at base, an economic analysis. Yet if these issues come to the fore, they will have an impact on the nature of the breakup and, therefore, will spill over into nature of the post-Canada economic environment for both Quebec and "the Rest of Canada" (ROC).

There are two additional economic perspectives that can be employed by those who tend to dismiss the threat that Quebec will leave. The first of these is that Quebec's success story on the economic front during the 1980s was largely a Montreal story. Specifically, in some of Quebec's regions — the Gaspésie, for example — earned incomes are still among the lowest in the country. A not insignificant factor that allowed Quebec to direct attention toward Montreal and vicinity was that Ottawa (and ROC) conveniently assumed the lion's share of supporting these lagging regions, either through unemployment insurance or through various regional development schemes.[1] Under independence, this distributional responsibility would fall to Quebec and would complicate further an already challenging transition.

The second perspective is more general in that it encompasses the first: namely, that societal revolutions are almost invariably elitist. As Albert Breton noted more than 25 years ago in the introduction to his now-classic paper on the economics of nationalism:

> It is the object of this paper, first, to show that societies in which political nationalism exists invest resources in nationality or ethnicity; second, that these investments are made because they are profitable; and third, that they are not profitable for everyone in a society but only for specific and identifiable groups. Taken together, the second and third points mean that investments in nationality are not so much income-creating as income-redistributing.[2]

Breton went on to point out that:

> The monetary rate of return on this capital takes the form of high-income jobs for the nationals of a given territory. We have also seen that from a social point of view the rate of return in terms of income on this form of capital is lower than if resources were economically invested in alternative uses. The question that comes to mind then is: Why does society invest in nationality or ethnicity? The answer is to be found in the income redistributing effect of these investments, an answer which is already implicit in the foregoing discussion. For even if these investments have a low yield, this yield accrues to a specific

---

1 See Thomas J. Courchene, *What Does Ontario Want?* (Toronto: York University, Robarts Centre for Canadian Studies, 1989).

2 Albert Breton, "The Economics of Nationalism," *Journal of Political Economy* 72 (1964): 376.

group in society even though that group pays only for a fraction
of the cost of the investment.[3]

The inevitable redistribution could — and presumably would,
to a degree — be toward francophone Quebecers from other groups
in Quebec society. But since these latter groups are generally quite
mobile and since sovereignty is, from my vantage point at least, a
negative-sum game, it is difficult to avoid the conclusion that there
would be considerable redistribution *within* Québécois society. On
this score, I do not think that one should spend too much time
worrying about the economic future within an independent Quebec
of the members of the Bélanger-Campeau Commission. Theory suggests that their *relative* income position within Quebec likely would
be enhanced and, perhaps, so might their *absolute* income position.
This implies that the "average" Quebecer would bear the brunt of
the costs of separation. This is a point worth emphasizing in both
Quebec and ROC: the economic casualties in any rending of
Canada's political integrity would not be the elites of either society.

Not surprisingly, perhaps, this conception of winners and losers
is beginning to play some role in the constitutional debate. Specifically, the argument goes that once the "average" Quebecer realizes
that the costs of achieving sovereignty would come out of his or her
pocketbook, attitudes toward sovereignty will change. Intriguingly,
however, this redistributional implication of sovereignty *is* beginning to be appreciated within Quebec. In his expert testimony before
the Bélanger-Campeau Commission, François Vaillancourt offered
the suggestion, perhaps tongue-in-cheek, that if independence or
sovereignty is inevitable, then it may be appropriate that civil
servants' salaries be pared back in the short term and the proceeds
distributed to those who are most likely to bear the brunt of separation.[4] Pierre Fortin made essentially the same point, but in a quite

---

3 Ibid., p. 379.

4 François Vaillancourt, "Réponses aux questions posées par la Commission sur
   l'avenir politique et constitutionnel du Québec," in Quebec, Commission on the
   Political and Constitutional Future of Quebec [Bélanger-Campeau Commission],
   Les avis des spécialistes invités à répondre aux huit questions posées par la Commission
   [Background papers], vol.4 (Quebec, 1991), p. 1125.

different manner. His argument was that the Quebec economy in its social cohesion is more European than North American and, as a result, there would be a concerted societal effort to make independence "work", if independence is in the cards.[5]

Recent actions by the Quebec government and Quebec labor are fully consistent with these observations. Quebec was quick off the mark to follow Ottawa's lead and cap the salaries of its civil servants — who, in Quebec, include academics. More recently still, one Quebec union, encouraged by the government, agreed to a strike-free six-year contract to entice Sammi of Korea to invest a half-billion dollars in its Atlas steel plant just outside Montreal and in the process to move its Canadian headquarters from Ontario to Quebec. This is viewed as a critical turning point in Quebec's socio-economic evolution. In a recent address to the Montreal Chamber of Commerce, Quebec's Minister of Industry, Trade and Technology, Gérald Tremblay, hailed this agreement as ushering in Quebec's "new social contract," involving as it does not only job creation, but also a new headquarters, a research center, enhanced secondary manufacturing, and a focus on skills enhancement. Tremblay concluded his Chamber of Commerce address with what he referred to as "the big question": "Do you have the will to succeed, not only as individuals but also as members of the Quebec collectivity?"[6] In an important sense, therefore, Quebec society has already begun to think and act with a post-Canada mentality. Intriguingly, this would also serve Quebec well within a renewed federalism!

The rest of Canada, however, appears to be completely unaware that this same redistributional proposition would apply to it as well. Creating a distinct entity in ROC certainly would privilege elites there, particularly unilingual elites. But ROC, too, would be engaged

---

5 Pierre Fortin, "Le choix forcé du Québec: aspects économiques et stratégiques," in Quebec, Commission on the Political and Constitutional Future of Quebec [Bélanger-Campeau Commission], *Les avis des spécialistes invités à répondre aux huit questions posées par la Commission* [Background papers], vol.4 (Quebec, 1991).

6 Translated from Gérald Tremblay, "Les entreprises doivent créer un nouveau modèle de succès au Québec," *La Presse* (Montreal), April 17, 1991, p. B3.

in a negative-sum economic game if Quebec were to separate. More-over, ROC appears to be tackling it "American-style", where lower-income Canadians likely are unaware that the new ROC would be built on their backs.

Now that I have broached the subject of the potential costs to the rest of Canada of a rending of the national fabric, I want to focus on a few aspects in more detail.

Suppose Quebec Goes?

The entrée into this discussion is to assume that, for whatever reason, Quebec opts for independence. Moreover, assume that a Canada-Quebec economic and monetary union is not in the cards, but that free trade agreements (FTAs) between Quebec and both the United States and ROC are successfully negotiated. I will further assume that the separation is reasonably friendly — readers who prefer to adopt the position that the breakup would be acrimonious can simply "ratchet up" what follows by a magnitude or so. The final assumption is that I shall focus on the position of Ontario.

Two background implications must be put on the table. First, as revealed by its recent budget, Ontario's deficit for fiscal year 1991/92 is forecast to be roughly $10 billion, over three times as large as the current deficit and, indeed, as any in its previous history. Moreover, projections are that the deficit is structural, in the sense that in fiscal year 1994/95 the estimated deficit will still be above $7 billion. This has dramatic implications for the current constitu-tional debate. Much of the "bon voyage" or "let Quebec go" move-ment in ROC assumes that Ontario, along with British Columbia and Alberta, would continue to play the role of ROC "paymasters" in terms of maintaining interregional transfers. The six ROC "have-not" provinces must surely be rethinking all of this in light of the Ontario budget.

The second implication is this: While one may not want to overlay cyclical and policy issues with the constitutional question, it has to be pointed out that Ontario's economy is on precarious ground. It is "hollowing out" and bleeding at the borders under the external effects of the recession, federal interest-rate and exchange-rate policies, the goods and services tax, and the internal or self-imposed consequences of an already unfavorable tax environment *vis-à-vis* the United States, soon to be made worse by Ontario's debt and deficit overhang. Part of the "soon-to-be-made-worse" scenario is the fact that unless combined Ontario and federal taxes fall more into line internationally, Ontario's tax base will begin to "migrate". This is the current backdrop not only for an exit by Quebec but also for the prospects of ROC's surviving as a single, united entity.

What, then, would Ontario's concerns be? The first is that neither the Canada-U.S. FTA nor the auto pact likely would remain intact — the latter because Ontario could no longer deliver the Quebec market and the former because the move from a bilateral to a multilateral FTA would give the United States an opening to renegotiate the present FTA.

Second, some proportion of the trade between Quebec and Ontario would be disrupted. How much is not, at this point, knowable. The expectation is that Quebec would come out distinctly second best, since the net migration of people and headquarters would be toward Ontario. Indeed, it is not difficult to conjure up scenarios wherein Ontario would also be inundated by migrants from Atlantic Canada, particularly since cuts in federal-provincial transfers in the past two federal budgets have left the future of social programs in those provinces in considerable doubt. To this "push" phenomenon one must add the "pull" of Ontario, now that it has staked out its position as Canada's social policy leader.

Third, if Quebec's economic situation deteriorated substantially, this would, of necessity, reflect on both Ontario and ROC in terms of credit ratings in international capital markets, particularly since Canada's debt would remain ROC's official responsibility. If the economic situation in Quebec dictated an inevitable reneging on its debt-sharing obligations to ROC, this would get reflected, internationally, as a ROC problem.

Fourth, in terms of putting "new Canada" together again, the six "have-not" provinces, as already alluded to, would want some commitment from Ontario, Alberta, and British Columbia to continue to underwrite the equalization system.

Fifth, all other provinces, particularly Alberta and British Columbia, would want some checks and balances — a Triple-E Senate or a severing of Ontario into, say, three provinces — to prevent Ontario's more than 50 percent (after the in-migration) of the population from dominating ROC.

At what point do Ontarians move to pursue their own self-interest? After all, a separate Ontario would make much more sense, economically, than a separate Quebec, particularly if Ontario could get some sort of "deal" with the United States on autos. There has been a great deal of discussion as to whether Quebec is a net beneficiary of Confederation in the narrow sense of dollar inflows and outflows. Yet there is no question about Ontario's position: in 1988 alone, it was a net contributor to the tune of between $831 and $1,035 per capita, depending on how the deficit is allocated,[7] or somewhere between $8 and $10 billion in nominal terms. One can throw in another $2 billion for the net outflows associated with the operations of unemployment insurance. While Alberta and British Columbia are also net contributors — in this narrow "balance-sheet" approach — the point for Ontario is simply that its budget would be in surplus over the next four years in the absence of outflows of these magnitudes, instead of rolling up a projected $35 billion in debt.

Sooner or later, these factors will begin to come to the fore, especially as Ontario contemplates further tax hikes over the next few years. This may be exacerbated in any breakup scenario if other provinces were to pressure Ontario to take an uncompromising stance — and one counter to its own self-interest — toward Quebec. Combined with the earlier comments about the province's competitiveness, the choice for Ontario would be to trigger this self-interest or face a hemorrhaging of economic activity toward the south. In other words, at what point would looking south or asserting its

---

7 See Isabella D. Horry and Michael A. Walker, *Government Spending Facts* (Vancouver: Fraser Institute, 1991), Tables 3.7 and 3.8.

dominance in the federation make a lot more sense for Ontario than looking west and (leapfrog-style) looking east? Or, if the focus is still east-west, at what point would Ontario insist that the interregional transfer system become effectively emasculated or "Americanized" — presumably with support on this issue from Alberta and British Columbia?

Note that the message here is not that Ontario and ROC generally do not desire to constitute or reconstitute a new Canada. No doubt they do. Rather, the underlying message is that the march of events on the economic front might be such as to overwhelm the values that bind Canadians in ROC together. It really does not matter how ROC governments or citizens *feel* about designing a Canada without Quebec. What matters is getting the *economics* on side, because if this does not materialize the tax base would simply migrate. And on this score, Ontario is far more vulnerable than either Alberta or British Columbia. In fact, it is far from axiomatic that a nine-province ROC would rise from the rubble of a rending of Canada's political integrity. Moreover, if it does, it would almost certainly be a much different country than exists in the minds of those ROC Canadians who have bought into the "let Quebec go" mentality.

Two conclusions derive from all of this. The first is that if ROC is intent on digging in its heels in terms of accommodating Quebec, then this strategy has to be backed up *in advance* with a substantial research effort on both the political/constitutional *and* economic fronts, replete with a series of agreed-on contingency plans if economic prospects deteriorate markedly.

The second conclusion is perhaps the more important. If ROC is intent on creating a society in its own likeness, it behooves us to shift away from the emotional plane to the strategic plane, and to begin asking the question of whether this new vision of ROC can also be created if Quebec *stays* in Confederation, thereby avoiding the potential for dysfunction on the economic front.

My answer for ROC is the same as it was for Quebec: ROC's economic and political/cultural future is best assured within a renewed federalism. Addressing the potential for a renewed federalism as a first-best option for the northern half of North America is the role of the final chapter.

Chapter 8

Renewed Federalism:
Opportunities and Prospects

Sorting Out the Issues:
A Probabilistic Approach

One way to approach the underlying challenge facing Canadians —
in particular, those in "the Rest of Canada" (ROC) — is to cast the
options in a probabilistic framework. This may not advance the
likelihood of a successful resolution, but it may serve to pinpoint the
nature of the underlying issues. What are the costs, in an expected-
value sense, of Quebec's leaving? These can be expressed as the
product of (a) the probability of its leaving and (b) the expected cost
to ROC if Quebec does leave. This value can then be matched with
the costs of accommodating Quebec's desires, which would be the
expected costs that ROC would bear because it would be "forced off"
its preferred conception of what "Canada" ought to be.

In an important sense, the societal debate in ROC revolves
around assessing the "costs" associated with Quebec's leaving or
staying. In terms of the former, my personal evaluation is that the
costs are likely to be very high on the economic front and fairly
significant on the political front as well — that is, in terms of ROC's
ability to remain a single society or country.

For some ROC citizens, these costs are assumed to be "negative" — that is, they are in the nature of gains, since the assumptions
are that (a) the economic costs are insignificant and (b) the "gain"
from having Quebec out of the picture would be an opportunity to
design a "preferable" nation. Almost axiomatically, this group of
Canadians would opt for nonaccommodation, since the impact of

Quebec's staying would presumably be a Canada that no longer resonated with Quebec's aspirations. Intriguingly, the worst possible outcome for this group would be nonaccommodation followed by a decision by Quebec to *stay* in Canada; in such a case, not only would these Canadians be frustrated from achieving their "new" ROC, but they might also have to settle for a Canada in which Quebec was even more entangled, particularly if Quebecers continue to "block vote" or, equivalently, to vote "Bloc".

For another group of Canadians, perhaps the majority, there are costs to both options. An exit by Quebec would be costly, but so would be an accommodation of Quebec's demands. These are really the "swing" Canadians who presumably will determine the future of this country. As the constitutional debate unfolds, they will be influenced on the one hand by the perceived costs to ROC of Quebec's leaving and on the other hand by the nature of the accommodation necessary to keep Quebec "in the fold".

Finally, there is the group to which I belong — and which I hope numbers more than one. This group views renewed federalism as the first-best option. One aspect of this is the belief, outlined in the previous chapters of this study, that a rending of Canada's political integrity would be very costly — certainly from an economic standpoint, and potentially from a political one as well. The critical first-best aspect to my approach is that I believe that renewed federalism has the greatest potential for enhancing the economic prospects *and* the "political" desires of both Quebec and ROC. Thus, in this concluding chapter, I want to attempt to make the case that renewed federalism can be a first-best option.

There are several strands to the analysis, not all of which can be elaborated in appropriate detail. Foremost among these is to recognize that Quebec's "demands" constitute two quite separate thrusts. The first is the desire for enhanced powers, largely but not exclusively, in the area of "demolinguistics" — immigration, language, and culture — along with more powers in the areas of communications, postsecondary education, skills training, unemployment insurance, regional development, and research and development.

These are the issues with which Canadians in ROC are preoccupied, since they likely imply a reworking of the division of federal-provincial powers within Confederation.

The second thrust — which really dominates the Allaire Report — is that the global economic community is passing Canada by. The Canadian federation is faltering economically. It is too "entangled" in some areas, unable at the federal level to control deficits, poorly structured in terms of the relationship of the Bank of Canada to the federal government, Canadians are overgoverned, and on and on. Quebec, on the other hand, perceives itself — perhaps wrongly — as a "winner" on the economic front over the 1980s and wants to be part of a federation that, at the center, also acts in ways that allow Canadians to "win". In this sense, Quebec's challenge to ROC is to reconstitute itself — along with Quebec — in a manner consistent with benefiting from the ongoing and inevitable globalization, rather than fighting rearguard skirmishes that leave Canada falling behind its trading partners. As I noted at the beginning of this study, this is the "opportunity" aspect of the ongoing challenge — an opportunity for all Canadians to rethink and restructure how, as a society, they ought to position themselves in the emerging global reality.

Canadians in ROC will go a long way toward addressing Quebec's overall demands if they can respond to this economic challenge. Indeed, part of the distance has been traveled already. In a sense, aspects of the Quebec challenge began to be addressed, at long last, in the two most recent federal budgets — for example, public sector wages have been capped, spending guidelines will be legislated, and the federal debt and deficit issue has been joined with the proceeds of the goods and services tax to be devoted to debt servicing. To be sure, much of this has been accomplished on the backs of the provinces. The popular view is that the Mulroney government is reacting to, and attempting to undercut, the Reform Party. An equally valid view is that Ottawa is implementing important aspects of the Allaire Report, particularly in terms of the federal government's disentanglement from social programs. All that remains is to transfer some tax points to the provinces.

Nevertheless, Canadians' attention remains riveted on the political and constitutional thrust of Quebec's demands — namely, its desire for greater powers within the federation. As I noted above, the argument that a renewed federalism is the first-best option implies that a reworking of the approach to federalism can accommodate Quebec and at the same time fulfill important aspirations of ROC. In order to address this, I want first to focus briefly on a series of external forces and factors that will lead to a rethinking and, indeed, a restructuring of major aspects of the Canadian federation irrespective of the past or future of relations between Quebec and ROC.

Forces Impinging on the Canadian Federation

Globalization

Globalization and the telecommunications revolution are affecting the role of national governments in at least four ways.[1] Two of these relate to a transfer "upward" of some of the traditional powers of the nation-state.

The first is the growing importance of *transnational* corporations. Unlike *multinational* corporations, which entered countries subject to a host of "commitments", transnationals increasingly enter under conditions of "national treatment" — that is, treatment on a par with national corporations. This has substantial implications. For example, one will no longer be able to speak meaningfully about a "national" production economy; instead, production increasingly will be international. One obvious consequence is that much of the welfare state will have to be rethought and reworked, since national welfare states are in large measure geared to national production machines.

Second, it is the transnational corporation — the international private sector — not the international public sector, that is driving

---

1 This section is from Thomas J. Courchene, *Global Competitiveness and the Canadian Federation* (Toronto: C.D. Howe Institute, forthcoming).

globalization. What this means is that national governments increasingly will find that activities that used to be done at the national level will now have to be passed "upward", partly as a countervail to the globalizing transnationals. The Bank for International Settlements' capital-adequacy rules for financial institutions are a good example here. More than a dozen nations have committed themselves to abide by these international standards. Moreover, the European Community (EC) itself is probably part of this trend, particularly if it initiates Community-wide taxation in the area, say, of corporate income taxation. This trend toward international regulation, international standards, and confederal or EC-type arrangements is bound to expand and multiply.

Two other forces are passing power "downward" from nation-states. First, globalization and the information revolution are empowering citizens. There are many facets to this. For example, as recent as a decade ago, "transmitters" determined the information flow; increasingly "receptors" will do so. Indeed, the thesis of Kenichi Ohmae's current bestseller, *The Borderless World*, as outlined on the book's dustjacket, is that globalization is really about consumer sovereignty: "performance standards are now set in the global marketplace by those that buy the products, not those that make them or regulate them." Quebecers are all too aware of this trend in light of the restrictions placed by Vermont on a recent sale by Hydro-Québec to that state. The essential point is that consumers — individually and as part of local, national, or international groups of like-minded citizens — are exerting substantial power, which will surely complicate old-style governance for unitary and federal states alike.

A second and more intriguing way in which power is being passed downward from nation-states is the spread of globalization across the world through a network of "international" cities. These cities — Montreal, Toronto, and Vancouver for Canada — are the critical national nodes in global communications and trading networks. In the terminology used by Jane Jacobs, they are the essential cultural and economic "connectors" outward to other international cities such as Frankfurt and Geneva and inward to places such as

Kingston and Sherbrooke. Over the past decade, nothing much has changed in terms of the Ottawa-Paris relationship, but much has changed in terms of the Montreal-Paris relationship. The dilemma here for Canadian federalism is obvious: Montreal, Toronto, and Vancouver are "constitutionless"; they are creatures of their respective provincial governments, but they will soon become much more influential. This poses rather unique problems because, for example, the international city for Saskatchewan (Vancouver) is not located in the province and the international city for the Maritime provinces (arguably, Boston) is not even in the same country. This again poses constraints on the role and influence of national, even provincial, governments. Intriguingly, but not surprisingly, Metro Toronto recently proposed that these three cities be given "provincial" status in any reworking of the Constitution.

I shall limit myself to only one implication from all of this. In the face of a diminished role in the economic, regulatory, and even cultural sphere for national governments, citizens increasingly will view "sovereignty" as the ability to have some influence on how they live and work and play. One can argue whether the appropriate level of government to deliver this is the international city or the provincial government or the local government, but under Canada's federal system it is clearly *not* the national government. Indeed, will there be much left of "sovereignty" in the new century other than distinct societies?

It is difficult to avoid the conclusion that these global forces are inherently decentralizing in terms of the internal workings of Confederation. Canadians, particularly those in ROC, may desire a strong federal government, but this has to be a "new" sort of government, with a greater emphasis on securing an internal economic union or overseeing a new "social contract".

Fiscal-Driven Decentralization

The two most recent federal budgets have had the effect of driving Canada toward unprecedented decentralization, particularly in the area of social programs. Leading the way is the five-year cap on the total of Established Programs Financing (EPF). What this means in practice is that Ottawa's EPF cash transfers will fall to zero in a couple of years for Quebec and early in the next century for the rest of the provinces. For the richer provinces, the growth in Canada Assistance Plan payments has been capped at 5 percent. Finally, the ceiling is binding on equalization, so that for the current year payments are more than $1 billion lower than they would have been if there were no ceiling.

In tandem, this amounts to a dramatic decentralization in terms of federal-provincial finances. Indeed, one could argue that Canada is in the midst of its most profound *de facto* change in the division of powers, since changes in the magnitude and nature of these intergovernmental grants are tantamount to changes in the division of powers themselves.

Partly in response to the fiscal pressures that Ottawa is unloading on the provinces, it is now contemplating allowing the ROC provinces much more flexibility in terms of the joint personal income tax (PIT) system. Specifically, the 1991 federal budget indicates that Ottawa will look seriously at granting the provinces the ability to apply their own rate and bracket structures to the commonly determined tax base.

The provinces are also responding to this crunch. Meeting in Lloydminster, Sask., last July, the premiers of the four western provinces talked seriously about a separate PIT for western Canada. In the east, the initiatives relating to Maritime economic union are not independent of the very serious fiscal pressure that those provinces will come under in the next few years.

The Free Trade Agreement

Economic activity was progressively shifting from east-west to north-south well before the Canada-U.S. Free Trade Agreement (FTA) was implemented. What this suggests is that the political economy of the east-west transfer system will fall under increasing scrutiny in the context of north-south integration. In particular, Ontario's "magnanimity" in terms of existing regional transfers historically carried a healthy dose of "Ontario first". As long as trade flowed largely east-west, with Ontario being the principal north-south conduit, the second- (and future-) round spending impacts of these regional transfers generally came to rest somewhere in Ontario. Under enhanced north-south integration for Canada's provinces, the second-round spending may end up in North Carolina or California. At a political level, this will begin to erode support for regional transfers, particularly those that privilege "place" rather than people. The FTA may enhance these pressures, but they were mounting in any event.

Summary

Globalization, decentralization, and free trade, then, are introducing profound changes. None of them has anything to do with Meech Lake. But the Meech Lake debate — and now the post-Meech Lake debate — is serving to mask their reality for many Canadians. Nonetheless, these factors will perforce alter the Canadian federation as we approach the millennium.

I draw three observations from this. First, it will inevitably alter the role of national governments. The old centralization/decentralization debate is largely sterile for those areas where the global economy is now the driving force: it does not matter nearly as much as it used to who holds these powers, since they will follow global dictates.

The second observation is that some "rebalancing" of powers is probably in order as a result of the interplay of these forces. Let me focus on just two areas. The first of these relates to policy priorities as a result of globalization and the telecommunications revolution. Increasingly, knowledge is at the cutting edge of competitiveness. This implies that an emphasis on human-capital formation, skills training, research and development, and the like will become increasingly critical to the success of Canada and Canadians in the emerging global reality. There probably needs to be a greater national commitment to ensure equality of opportunity in terms of acquiring and enhancing Canadians' human capital. This may or may not require increased federal powers, but it probably does require greater federal leadership.

The other area in which some rebalancing of powers is probably necessary relates to social policy. The challenge facing all nations is how to devise a social contract consistent with global integration. What bound Canadians together, east-west, in the early years were economic policies such as the tariff, the railroads, and the range of other initiatives that has come to be known as the "National Policy". In a sense, Canadians utilized these economic levers to redistribute income east-west and away from the United States. The FTA, and integration generally, implies that economic levers can no longer be used largely for purposes of income redistribution. Moreover, precious little on the economic front binds Canadians east-west.[2] Rather, Canada's new "National Policy"[3] is a "social policy railroad".

Yet, as noted earlier, much of the federal-provincial transfer system that underlay this social policy infrastructure is now in shambles. Clearly, part of any reconstituted federalism will have to address this issue, perhaps to the point of developing some national principles relating to a new social contract. This is particularly important for some of the "have-not" provinces, since they will be loathe to accept any accommodation of Quebec's demands without some adequate federal-provincial social safety net in place. The fact that they may be worse off if Quebec leaves than they would be under a renewed federalism is somewhat beside the point: they too want to see renewed federalism as an attractive option. As the above analysis suggested, however, it is unlikely that this new social contract would be as generous to the provinces or as riddled with inappropriate incentives as that which passes for the status quo.

---

2 See Thomas J. Courchene and John N. McDougall, "The Context for Future Constitutional Options," in Ronald L. Watts and Douglas M. Brown, eds., *Options for a New Canada* (Toronto: University of Toronto Press, 1991), pp. 33–52.

3 Hinted at nearly 40 years ago by Vernon C. Fowke, "The National Policy — Old and New," *Canadian Journal of Economics and Political Science* 18 (August 1952): 27–86.

The third observation I want to make is that many of Quebec's demands are fully consistent with emerging global trends. It would be the height of folly steadfastly to reject Quebec's requests, only to find a few years down the road that ROC has to implement similar measures.

Thus, the possibility that renewed federalism is a first-best option on the political and constitutional front centers around two features:

- First, a rebalancing or reworking of institutional arrangements is eminently achievable *within* the federation because it will be done within the context of a positive-sum economic game.
- Second, the range of instruments for rearranging the federation is so large and so flexible that there are plenty of ways to accommodate the desires of both ROC and Quebec.

I recognize that it is with respect to this last point that I differ from many, perhaps most, of my fellow Canadians in ROC. The general view is that ROC's politics, culture, and identity would be diminished if Quebec is accommodated. In my view, however, this is wrong. I believe that ROC, Quebec, and Canada can *all* be enriched by a creative rethinking and reworking of institutional and constitutional arrangements.

In Praise of Renewed Federalism

There are probably as many visions of what a renewed federalism might look like as there are Canadians. And over the next year and a half there may be nearly as many proposals. My distinct preference is for what I have called "The Community of the Canadas."[4] Here, however, I do not want to argue for any particular model. Rather, I

---

4 Thomas J. Courchene, "The Community of the Canadas" (Kingston, Ont., Queen's University, Institute of Intergovernmental Relations, 1991). The French version of this paper appears in the volume of background papers to the Bélanger-Campeau Report.

want to focus on the incredible variety of instruments that are available for redesigning the Canadian federation. I also want to do something clearly un-Canadian by celebrating past accomplishments in terms of just how creative and adept we were (and still can be!) as a federal nation living and working within the existing Constitution.

Some reflection on aspects of these past achievements is an appropriate way to start. First, Canada was able to undergo vast swings in terms of decentralization and centralization without much, if any, change to the *Constitution Act, 1867*. Thus, there was centralization during wartime, then decentralization during the prosperous 1960s and early 1970s, then renewed centralization for the next decade. Decentralization now seems to be where we are headed — or, perhaps more correctly, rebalancing — once more.

Second, Canadians have been innovative in a great number of areas. Several examples come to mind. The initial equalization program was a product of ordinary federal legislation. It became such a hallmark of Canadian federation that the principle was enshrined in the *Constitution Act, 1982*. Saddled with a Senate that was potentially powerful but that lacked the moral authority to exercise this power, Canadians developed "executive federalism" — at the apex of which is the First Ministers' Conference — which allowed some way of bringing provincial input to decisions at the center and vice versa. My colleague Ed Safarian refers to executive federalism as Canada's "contribution to the art of federalism."[5] To be sure, executive federalism has fallen on hard times recently, particularly in the Meech Lake process, but this merely implies that it is time to become creative again.

Third, Canadians are pioneers in the development of parliamentary democracy: the Charter of Rights and Freedoms was introduced within a parliamentary framework. The Charter is, in my view, a remarkable achievement in its own right.

---

5 A.E. Safarian, *Ten Markets or One? Regional Barriers to Economic Activity* (Toronto: Ontario Economic Council, 1980), p. 18.

Fourth, rather than change the formal allocation of powers, Canadians have used the intergovernmental transfer system to change *de facto* powers. An emphasis on unconditional grants enhances provincial powers, while conditional grants and the use of the spending power increase federal authority. In the process, so-called national programs were created — provincially run programs in health and social assistance that became "national" by virtue of their portability, accessibility, lack of residency requirements, and the like.

Fifth, Canadians also did some rather mundane but important things, such as formally changing the division of powers between the federal and provincial governments. For example, constitutional amendments gave old age pensions and unemployment insurance to the federal government. Somewhat more creatively, the public pension system was made "concurrent with provincial paramountcy" — a concept that I will feature later — which meant that Quebec could initiate its own pension plan and which made it possible for ROC to allow Ottawa to mount the Canada Pension Plan on behalf of non-Quebecers.

Sixth, Canadians have always found ways to allow for diversity. In this context, the most creative instrument has been "opting out". Quebec controls several program areas that the other provinces have left to Ottawa. Along similar lines, Quebec has its own PIT, while ROC has a shared PIT with Ottawa. Here is a case where allowing Quebec to "opt out", also allowed ROC to have a far more harmonized system than if Quebec were required to remain in.

There are many other examples of ways in which Canadians have been innovative in addressing their constitutional and institutional needs, but by now the point should be obvious. Canadians have displayed a rare genius in accommodating their political structure to internal and external forces. Moreover, it is important to recognize that most of these innovations *did not require a formal constitutional amendment*, even though they affected the *de facto* division of powers between Ottawa and the provinces

The challenge Canadians now face is once again to call on this innate ability to adjust institutions to emerging needs. To some degree, this challenge can be met by deploying the current array of instruments more creatively. What is encouraging, however, is that further novel instruments are coming to the fore.

Among the most promising of these new instruments is "concurrency", which would allow both levels of government to legislate in certain areas.[6] Canada's Constitution, unlike that of many other countries, has very few concurrent powers. Yet almost all policy areas end up *de facto* being concurrent.

One approach to concurrency is to associate it with provincial paramountcy. "Concurrency with provincial paramountcy" (or CPP for short) is the principal operational instrument driving my "Community of the Canadas". It would give Quebec access to more powers while still allowing Ottawa to legislate in these areas. Quebec wants greater control of culture, for example, but it appears to be quite satisfied with such national institutions as the research councils and the National Film Board, so it likely would accept federal legislation in these areas.

Under CPP, the other provinces would be entirely free to rebalance, to decentralize, or to centralize — the same freedom they would have if Quebec left the federation, but without the economic costs of such an exit. Moreover, section 94 of the Constitution could come into play here. Essentially, this allows the non-Quebec provinces to coordinate (or "to pass up" to Ottawa) their powers in the general area of property and civil rights. According to Frank Scott, section 94 was included so that, in a more favorable political climate than that of 1864–66, it would afford an easy way for closer integration of the non-Quebec provinces.[7] In tandem, CPP and section 94 allow "symmetry" — or equality of the provinces — in principle and "asymmetry" in practice.

---

6 For further discussions of concurrency, see Courchene, "The Community of the Canadas"; and David Milne, "Equality or Asymmetry: Why Choose?" in Watts and Brown, eds., *Options for a New Canada*.

7 Quoted in Samuel LaSelva, "Federalism and Unanimity: The Supreme Court and Constitutional Amendment," *Canadian Journal of Political Science* 16 (December 1983): 757–770.

Effectively, the PIT is concurrent. Ottawa controls its own part,[8] while the provinces' part is really operated under CPP. At any point, any province can follow Quebec's lead and set up its own personal income tax. In a way, the RCMP operates under CPP as well: in terms of provincial policing, the provinces can opt to "hire" the RCMP or, if they wish, follow the lead of Quebec and Ontario and establish their own provincial police forces.

There is another powerful instrument that, while not new, might also play a key role this time around — namely, the economic union. If decentralization in some areas is inevitable, an enhanced economic union, perhaps run through the Senate, might act as an appropriate counterweight.

As emphasized above, much can be done without touching the Constitution. For example, one of the key points in the Allaire Report is that the structure of the relationship between the federal government and the Bank of Canada ought to be changed to make the Bank more independent. David Laidler has recently addressed the pros and cons of developing for Canada a variant of the U.S. Federal Reserve approach, which would strengthen the independence of the Bank but which would also constrain the power of the governor of the Bank by strengthening the role of the directors of the Bank in policymaking.[9] This may or may not be desirable, but the federal government need only pass the necessary legislation to bring it about; it does not require a constitutional amendment.

Finally, but not exhaustively, the *Constitution Act, 1982* provides a mechanism for amending the Constitution that does not require

---

8 Although it did transfer an extra 16.5 points to Quebec, so that Quebecers pay less federal tax than do taxpayers in ROC, but this was to be offset by an equivalent decrease in cash transfers to Quebec. A problem may arise when EPF cash transfers fall to zero, since at the point Quebec will have more tax-point transfers than ROC. See Thomas J. Courchene and Arthur E. Stewart, "Provincial Personal Income Taxation and the Future of the Tax Collection Agreements," in Melville McMillan, ed., *Provincial Public Finances*, vol. 2, *Plaudits, Problems, and Prospects* (Toronto: Canadian Tax Foundation, 1991), pp. 266–300.

9 See David E.W. Laidler, *How Shall We Govern the Governor? A Critique of the Governance of the Bank of Canada*, The Canada Round 1 (Toronto: C.D. Howe Institute, 1991).

ratification by unaffected provinces. Specifically, section 43 of the act reads as follows:

> An amendment of the Constitution of Canada in relation to any provision that applies to one or more, but not all, provinces, including
>
> > a) any alterations to boundaries between provinces, and
> > b) any amendment to any provision that relates to the use of the English or the French language within a province,
>
> may be made by proclamation issued by the Governor General under the Great Seal of Canada only where so authorized by resolutions of the Senate and House of Commons and of the legislative assembly of each province to which the amendment applies.

The most ardent advocate of section 43 as the key to unlocking the constitutional impasse is probably Patrick Monahan of Osgoode Hall Law School. Monahan argues that this section is "the only realistic prospect for accomplishing constitutional changes to accommodate Quebec under the existing legal procedures." He goes on:

> Under section 43, it is possible for the federal Parliament and a single provincial legislature to enact an amendment without reference to the other provinces. Such an amendment must be limited to constitutional provisions that apply to "one or more, but not all, provinces." This somewhat limits the scope of any possible amendment utilizing this procedure. But it is noteworthy that a clause along the lines of the "distinct society" clause might have been enacted on the basis of the section 43 procedure.
>
> This possibility is reflected in the "Final Communiqué" issued by the First Ministers' Meeting on the Constitution, signed on 9 June 1990. The June 1990 agreement proposed a constitutional amendment that would have recognized that "within New Brunswick, the English linguistic community and the French linguistic community have equality of status and equal rights and privileges." The proposed amendment would also have affirmed the "role of the legislature and government of New Brunswick to preserve and promote the equality of status

and equal rights and privileges of the province's two official linguistic communities." In short, this proposed amendment tracked in fairly precise terms the "distinct society" clause in the Meech Lake Accord, with the exception that the amendment would have specified that it applied within New Brunswick alone. What is significant is that the June 1990 agreement specifically provided that this amendment would be enacted under the section 43 procedure, with only New Brunswick and Canada required to approve resolutions.[10]

Not all analysts would be as optimistic as Monahan in terms of the potential role for section 43, but it clearly and enhances the range of available instruments in a significant way.

While not in any way downplaying the magnitude of the post-Meech Lake societal challenge, it is equally important not to downplay the way in which the constitutional game has been played in the past nor to underestimate the incredible flexibility of the instruments that are available. There is, in my view, ample scope and flexibility to fashion a renewed federalism that will be first-best economically, politically, and constitutionally for both Quebec *and* ROC. There certainly is a way if there is a will.

Conclusion

I have argued in this study that Quebec independence *plus* an economic and monetary union between Quebec and Canada is neither feasible nor, over the longer term, desirable — either for Quebec or for Canada. If Quebec does leave, however, some arrangements would have to be made. The most likely of these would involve free trade agreements between Quebec and both the rest of Canada and the United States. It might also involve Quebec's "using" the Canadian dollar, at least initially. The difficulty with this scenario is that the transition period might be very costly and very

10 Patrick Monahan, *After Meech Lake: An Insider's View*, Reflections/Réflexions 5 (Kingston, Ont.: Queen's University, Institute of Intergovernmental Relations, 1990), p. 35.

lengthy, perhaps dramatically so. Moreover, it is not only Quebec that would suffer. ROC would too, perhaps to the point where its political integrity might be called into question.

For Quebec, both of these exit scenarios are quite inferior to a reconstituted federal system in which the province would achieve some greater powers, particularly in terms of what falls under the rubric of "demolinguistics".

For ROC, the conclusion is similar: a reconstituted or renewed federalism is the first-best option from an economic vantage point, and there is ample flexibility in terms of the instruments that are available to replicate virtually any structure that could come about from an independent ROC.

For Canadians generally, this moment represents an enormous opportunity. Quebec has alerted us to the need to restructure on the economic front in order to regain Canada's former competitive edge in the global economy. On the political and constitutional front, my plea is that Canadians begin to recognize that, as the second-largest federal nation in the world, Canada's diversity and complexity is only natural. If it is Quebec that feels economically and culturally constrained within Canada in the 1990s, then in the first decade of the 21st century it could be British Columbia that will want greater freedom and greater powers as it becomes more integrated with the Pacific Rim. If we cannot accommodate Quebec in 1992 then we probably will not be able to accommodate the western provinces in 2002. What we are addressing on the political and constitutional front, then, is really the way in which a regionally distinct but value-similar federation ought to evolve in the face of a rapidly changing global economic framework.

In my view, we have probably seen the apex of the emotional attachment to sovereignty in Quebec. If this is true, then the next year or so should see a Quebec more willing to remain in the Canadian fold. In the other provinces, the identification with a separate ROC, while less well developed than Quebecers' sense of self, is apparently still on the rise. Yet I am convinced that this, too, will turn around once Canadians understand the political and economic risks.

Virtually any vision of what this country ought to be in terms of how it affects me and my neighbors — whether in Kingston, Ontario, during the academic year or in Candle Lake, Saskatchewan, during the summer — can be achieved with Quebec's remaining in Canada. While it is still possible that unforseen actions on either side could rend the nation's political fabric, my best guess is that Canadians will opt for the first-best solution. All Canadians will want to embrace a Canada that reorganizes itself to be a "winner", since it is only within this context that Canadians can sustain the socio-cultural vision of their country that is gradually becoming the late 20th-century version of the last century's "national dream" of an east-west railway. Indeed, they will embrace such a Canada enthusiastically.

Bibliography

Boothe, Paul, and Richard Harris. "Alternative Divisions of Federal Assets and Liabilities." Paper presented to a conference on "Economic Dimensions of Constitutional Change," Kingston, Ont., John Deutsch Institute for the Study of Economic Policy, Queen's University, June 4–6, 1991.

Breton, Albert. "The Economics of Nationalism," *Journal of Political Economy* 72 (1964).

Canada. Parliament. Senate. Standing Committee on Banking, Trade and Commerce. *Canada 1992: Toward a National Market in Financial Services*, Eighth Report. Ottawa, 1990.

Chrétien, Jean. *Securing the Canadian Economic Union in the Constitution*. Ottawa: Supply and Services Canada, 1980.

Commission of the European Communities. "Draft Treaty Amending the Treaty Establishing the European Economic Community with a View to Achieving Economic and Monetary Union." Brussels, December 10, 1990.

———. *Economic and Monetary Union*. Brussels, 1990.

———. Directorate General for Economic and Financial Affairs. "One Market, One Money," *European Economy* 44 (October 1990).

Courchene, Thomas J. "The Community of the Canadas." Kingston, Ont., Queen's University, Institute of Intergovernmental Relations, 1991.

———. *Global Competitiveness and the Canadian Federation*. Toronto: C.D. Howe Institute, forthcoming.

———. *What Does Ontario Want?* Toronto: York University, Robarts Centre for Canadian Studies, 1989.

———. "Zero Means Almost Nothing: Towards a Preferable Inflation and Macroeconomic Policy," *Queen's Quarterly* 97 (1990).

———, and John N. McDougall. "The Context for Future Constitutional Options." In Ronald L. Watts and Douglas M. Brown, eds. *Options for a New Canada*. Toronto: University of Toronto Press, 1991.

———, and Arthur E. Stewart. "Provincial Personal Income Taxation and the Future of the Tax Collection Agreements." In Melville McMillan, ed. *Provincial Public Finances*, vol. 2, *Plaudits, Problems, and Prospects*. Toronto: Canadian Tax Foundation, 1991.

Dion, Léon. "Léon Dion propose un régime confédéral," *La Presse* (Montreal), January 11, 1991, p. B-3.

Fortin, Pierre. "Le choix forcé du Québec: aspects économiques et stratégiques." In Quebec, Commission on the Political and Constitutional Future of Quebec [Bélanger-Campeau Commission]. *Les avis des spécialistes invités à répondre aux huit questions posées par la Commission* [Background papers], vol.4. Quebec, 1991.

Fowke, Vernon C. "The National Policy — Old and New," *Canadian Journal of Economics and Political Science* 18 (August 1952).

Harris, Richard. "Post-Meech Economics: Some Observations." Department of Economics, Simon Fraser University, Burnaby, B.C., 1990, mimeographed.

Horry, Isabella D., and Michael A. Walker. *Government Spending Facts.* Vancouver: Fraser Institute, 1991.

Laidler, David E.W. *How Shall We Govern the Governor? A Critique of the Governance of the Bank of Canada,* The Canada Round 1. Toronto: C.D. Howe Institute, 1991.

LaSelva, Samuel. "Federalism and Unanimity: The Supreme Court and Constitutional Amendment," *Canadian Journal of Political Science* 16 (December 1983).

Latouche, Daniel. "La stratégie québécoise dans le nouvel ordre économique et politique international." In Quebec, Commission on the Political and Constitutional Future of Quebec [Bélanger-Campeau Commission]. *Les avis des spécialistes invités à répondre aux huit questions posées par la Commission* [Background papers], vol.4. Quebec, 1991.

Leslie, Peter. "Options for the Future of Canada: The Good, the Bad and the Fantastic." In Ronald L. Watts and Douglas M. Brown, eds. *Options for a New Canada.* Toronto: University of Toronto Press, 1990.

Mackenzie, Robert. "The Nation: Sovereignists Did Their Homework," *Toronto Star,* April 13, 1991, p. D4.

Melvin, James R. "Political Structure and the Pursuit of Economic Objectives." In Michael J. Trebilcock et al., eds. *Federalism and the Canadian Economic Union.* Toronto: Ontario Economic Council, 1983.

Milne, David. "Equality or Asymmetry: Why Choose?" In Ronald L. Watts and Douglas M. Brown, eds. *Options for a New Canada.* Toronto: University of Toronto Press, 1991.

Monahan, Patrick. *After Meech Lake: An Insider's View,* Reflections/Réflexions 5. Kingston, Ont.: Queen's University, Institute of Intergovernmental Relations, 1990.

Proulx, Pierre-Paul. "Un examin des échanges commerciaux du Québec avec les autres provinces canadiennes, les États-Unis et le reste du monde." In Quebec, Commission on the Political and Constitutional Future of Quebec [Bélanger-Campeau Commission]. *Éléments d'analyse économique pertinents à la révision du statut politique et constitutionnel du Québec* [Background papers], vol.1. Quebec, 1991.

Quebec. Commission on the Political and Constitutional Future of Quebec [Bélanger-Campeau Commission]. *Report* . Quebec, March 27, 1991.

Quebec Liberal Party. Constitutional Committee. *A Quebec Free to Choose* [Allaire Report]. Quebec, January 28, 1991.

Safarian, A.E. *Ten Markets or One? Regional Barriers to Economic Activity.* Toronto: Ontario Economic Council, 1980.

Soberman, Daniel. "European Integration: Are There Lessons for Canada?" In Ronald L. Watts and Douglas M. Brown, eds. *Options for a New Canada.* Toronto: University of Toronto Press, 1991.

Tremblay, Gérald. "Les entreprises doivent créer un nouveau modèle de succès au Québec," *La Presse* (Montreal), April 17, 1991, p. B3.

Tremblay, Rodrigue. "Le statut politique et constitutionnel du Québec." In Quebec, Commission on the Political and Constitutional Future of Quebec [Bélanger-Campeau Commission]. *Les avis des spécialistes invités à répondre aux huit questions posées par la Commission* [Background papers], vol.4. Quebec, 1991.

Vaillancourt, François. "Réponses aux questions posées par la Commission sur l'avenir politique et constitutionnel du Québec." In Quebec, Commission on the Political and Constitutional Future of Quebec [Bélanger-Campeau Commission]. *Les avis des spécialistes invités à répondre aux huit questions posées par la Commission* [Background papers], vol.4. Quebec, 1991.

Whalley, John. "Induced Distortions of Interprovincial Activity: An Overview of Issues." In Michael J. Trebilcock et al., eds. *Federalism and the Canadian Economic Union.* Toronto: Ontario Economic Council, 1983.

Members of the
C.D. Howe Institute*

---

* The views expressed in this publication are those of the author, and do not necessarily reflect the opinions of the Institute's members.

Coal Association of Canada
Confederation Life Insurance Company
Consumers Gas
Coopers & Lybrand
Glen H. Copplestone
E. Kendall Cork
Corporation du Groupe La Laurentienne
Coscan Development Corporation
William J. Cosgrove
Co-Steel Inc.
Pierre Côté
The Counsel Corporation
J.G. Crean
Crédit Lyonnais Canada
Crestbrook Forest Industries Ltd.
John Crispo
Crown Life Insurance Company Limited
Hugh A. Curtis
Cyanamid Canada Inc.
John G. Davis
Shirley Dawe
Deloitte & Touche
Desjardins, Ducharme
Desmarais Family Foundation
Robert Després
John H. Dickey
Digital Equipment of Canada Limited
William A. Dimma
Iain St. C. Dobson
Dofasco Inc.
The Dominion of Canada General
    Insurance Company
Domtar Inc.
Donohue Inc.
Dow Chemical Canada Inc.
Du Pont Canada Inc.
Edper Investments Ltd.
The Empire Life Insurance Company
Encor Inc.
Energy & Chemical Workers Union
H.E. English
Ernst & Young
Falconbridge Limited
Ronald J. Farano, Q.C.
John Farrow
Federal Industries Ltd.
Field & Field Perraton Masuch

Finning Ltd.
First Boston Canada
First Marathon Securities Limited
Fishery Products International Limited
Ford Motor Company of Canada, Limited
Formula Growth Limited
Four Seasons Hotels Limited
Donald T. Fudge
GSW Inc.
Gaz Métropolitain, Inc.
General Electric Canada Inc.
General Motors of Canada Limited
Gluskin Sheff + Associates Inc.
The Great-West Life Assurance Company
Morton Gross
Le Groupe Commerce, compagnie
    d'assurances
Groupe Sobeco Inc.
Gulf Canada Resources Limited
H. Anthony Hampson
C. Malim Harding Foundation
Hawker Siddeley Canada Inc.
J.-P. Hétu
Hewlett-Packard (Canada) Ltd.
Gordon Homer
Honeywell Limited
Hongkong Bank of Canada
Hydro-Québec
IBM Canada Ltd.
Imasco Limited
Imperial Oil Limited
Inco Limited
The Independent Petroleum Association
    of Canada
Inland Cement Limited
The Insurance Bureau of Canada
Interhome Energy Inc.
The Investors Group
IPSCO Incorporated
Tsutomu Iwasaki
John A. Jacobson
Jarislowsky, Fraser & Company
Robert Johnstone
John Labatt Limited
LAC Minerals Ltd.
R.William Lawson
Jacques Lefebvre

David Lewis
Gérard Limoges
Daniel Lobb
London Life Insurance Company
Pierre Lortie
J.W. (Wes) MacAleer
James McAlpine
McCallum Hill Companies
MacDonald, Dettwiler & Associates Ltd.
Robert M. MacIntosh
Bruce M. McKay
McKinsey & Company
Maclab Enterprises
James Maclaren Industries Inc.
Maclean-Hunter Limited
Charles McMillan
McMillan, Binch
MacMillan Bloedel Limited
Manufacturers Hanover Bank of Canada
The Manufacturers Life Insurance
    Company
Georg Marais
Maritime Telegraph & Telephone
    Company, Limited
Marsh & McLennan Limited
The Mercantile and General Reinsurance
    Company of Canada
William M. Mercer Limited
Merck Frosst Canada Inc.
Midland Walwyn Inc.
Miles Canada Inc.
Les Minoteries Ogilvie Ltée.
Robert Mitchell Inc.
Mitsui & Co. (Canada) Ltd.
The Molson Companies Limited
Monsanto Canada Inc.
Montréal Trust Company of Canada
Moore Corporation Limited
W.D. Mulholland
The Mutual Life Assurance Company of
    Canada
NCR Canada Ltd.
National Westminster Bank of Canada
Nesbitt Thomson Deacon
Peter C. Newman
Noranda Forest Inc.
Noranda Inc.
Norcen Energy Resources Limited

North American Life Assurance Company
North Canadian Oils Limited
Northern Telecom Limited
Northwood Pulp and Timber Limited
NOVA Corporation of Alberta
Ontario Hydro
The Oshawa Group Limited
PanCanadian Petroleum Limited
Peat Marwick Thorne
Lucie Pépin
Petro-Canada Inc.
Claude Pichette
Les Placements T.A.L. Ltée.
Placer Dome Inc.
Portfolio Management Corporation
David A. Potts
Power Corporation of Canada
Pratt & Whitney Canada Inc.
Price Waterhouse & Co.
J. Robert S. Prichard
Procor Limited
ProGas Limited
Provigo Inc.
Quebec and Ontario Paper Company
    Limited
RBC Dominion Securities Inc.
Redpath Industries Limited
Simon S. Reisman
Henri Remmer
Retail Council of Canada
Grant L. Reuber
R.T. Riley
Robin Hood Multifoods Inc.
Rogers Communications Inc.
Rothschild Canada Inc.
The Royal Bank of Canada
Royal Insurance Company of Canada
Royal Trust
St. Lawrence Cement Inc.
Sandwell Inc.
Saskoil
Guylaine Saucier
André Saumier
The Hon. Maurice Sauvé
Sceptre Investment Counsel
Sceptre Resources Limited
ScotiaMcLeod Inc.

Sears Can   n Bank
Hugh D. S   per Limited
Anthony
Sharwood
Shell Cana
Sherritt G
Sidbec-Do
Smith, Ly
    May
Le Soleil
Southam
Derek J. S
Standard
Stikeman
Strategicc
Sun Life
Suncor In
Swiss Bar
Teck Cor
Thomson
3M Cana

G. Arnold
David Ki
Paul H. L